Frances Tustin

This is the first book to describe the life and work of Frances Tustin, a brilliant clinician whose understanding of autistic and psychotic children has illuminated the relationship between autism and psychosis for others in the field.

Sheila Spensley defines Tustin's position in traditional and contemporary psychoanalytic theory and explains how it is related to work in infant psychiatry and developmental psychology. She clarifies key terms and concepts of her work, showing how they are linked with the work of Bion, and with that of Grotstein and Ogden. Evaluating autism from an evolutionary point of view, she also considers the possibility of autism as a 'missing link' in the developmental chain of psychic growth.

Frances Tustin makes Tustin's seminal work accessible to the non-specialist reader and shows how relevant her thinking is to work in other areas such as learning disability and work with adult patients.

Sheila Spensley is Consultant Clinical Psychologist and Psychoanalytic Psychotherapist at the Willesden Centre for Psychological Treatment, Willesden Community Hospital.

Sheila Spensley's *Frances Tustin* is a remarkable work: the author deftly interweaves a sensitively constructed personal account of the life of Frances Tustin with a detailed discussion of Tustin's major clinical and theoretical contributions to the psychoanalytic understanding and treatment of autistic patients.

Mrs Tustin's ideas and clinical approach are subtle and complex (often deceptively so). I have been richly rewarded by careful study of her work over the past fifteen years, but nonetheless came away from each chapter of Spensley's book feeling that I had learned something new and important about Tustin's thinking. Spensley, with clarity and unpretentious erudition, discusses such topics as Tustin's concepts of the sensation-dominated nature of autistic experience, the biological and interpersonal origins of autistic psychopathology, the unique quality of autistic anxiety, the differences between encapsulated and entangled forms of autism, the nature of 'relatedness' to autistic shapes and autistic objects. In each instance Spensley provides a rich commentary on the theoretical context for the idea under discussion as well as vivid clinical examples of the concept as Spensley has applied it in her own work.

Frances Tustin will be highly valued reading by all mental health practitioners and teachers (of every level of experience) who are attempting the difficult task of deepening their understanding of autistic patients as well as the autistic component of healthier patients.

Thomas H. Ogden, MD, Co-Director, Center for the Advanced Study of the Psychoses, San Francisco; Supervising and Training Analyst, Psychoanalytic Institute of Northern California; author of *The Primitive Edge of Experience*.

The Makers of Modern Psychotherapy
Series editor: Laurence Spurling

This series of introductory, critical texts looks at the work and thought of key contributors to the development of psychodynamic psycho-therapy. Each book shows how the theories examined affect clinical practice, and includes biographical material as well as a compre-hensive bibliography of the contributor's work.

The field of psychodynamic psychotherapy is today more fertile but also more diverse than ever before. Competing schools have been set up, rival theories and clinical ideas circulate. These different and sometimes competing strains are held together by a canon of fundamental concepts, guiding assumptions and principles of practice.

This canon has a history, and the way we now understand and use the ideas that frame our thinking and practice is palpably marked by how they came down to us, by the temperament and experiences of their authors, the particular puzzles they wanted to solve and the contexts in which they worked. These are the makers of modern psychotherapy. Yet despite their influence, the work and life of some of these eminent figures is not well known. Others are more familiar, but their particular contribution is open to reassessment. In studying these figures and their work, this series will articulate those ideas and ways of thinking that practitioners and thinkers within the psychodynamic tradition continue to find persuasive.

Laurence Spurling

Frances Tustin

Sheila Spensley

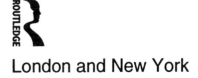

London and New York

First published 1995
by Routledge
11 New Fetter Lane, London EC4P 4EE

Simultaneously published in the USA and Canada
by Routledge
29 West 35th Street, New York, NY 10001

© 1995 Sheila Spensley

Typeset in Times by LaserScript, Mitcham, Surrey
Printed and bound in Great Britain by
Biddles Ltd, Guildford and King's Lynn

British Library Cataloguing in Publication Data
A catalogue record for this book is available from the British Library

Library of Congress Cataloging in Publication Data
A catalogue record for this book has been requested

ISBN 0–415–09262–0 (hbk)
ISBN 0–415–09263–9 (pbk)

To

Philip

Much analytic theory is not only compatible with, but derives some antecedent probability from, our beliefs about biology.

Money-Kyrle (1978)

I am convinced of the strength of the scientific position of psychoanalytic practice.

Bion (1962b)

Contents

Acknowledgements

The suggestion that I might write this book originated in conversations between Frances Tustin and Laurence Spurling, the editor of this series. It was a pleasure for me to accept the task of writing about an area of psychoanalytic investigation which has long been a particular interest and about a writer whose work has contributed substantially to my own understanding. Personal friendship with the subject of biographical work can present problems but in this case I think the strength of shared interests and priorities has fortified rather than interfered with objectivity and critical freedom. I am grateful to Frances Tustin for her generosity in making available to me as much as she could recover of her history and of her memories and for providing me with the manuscripts of some of her clinical work.

The research for the writing of the book has also brought unexpected pleasures in becoming an opportunity to renew old acquaintances and friendships and to make new ones. Pleasurable memories remain with me of a beautiful day at the New Forest home of Mrs Shirley Hoxter, retired Head of the Child and Family Department of the Tavistock Clinic, who gave her time to a careful reading of the first typescript and made a number of corrections and helpful suggestions.

I am grateful to Fiona Spensley Barton and to Melinda Schneider who read the chapters as they emerged, hot from the PC, and made constructive criticisms.

Thanks are due to Michael Sinason, former consultant psychotherapist at the Willesden Centre for Psychological Treatment, for first introducing me to computer technology. He was responsible for teaching me to become, much to my surprise, computer literate. Colin Spensley introduced the wonders of Windows and I am grateful also for his technological help and supervision which retrieved the book from many a threatened 'black hole'.

It would not have been possible to write this book at all without a substantial experience of working with deeply disturbed patients and it was my work with psychotic and borderline adult patients which interested me in the disturbances of childhood. I am ever grateful for the rare opportunity of having worked in one of the few NHS in-patient psychotherapy units, at Shenley Hospital, while it existed. With the demise of both this unit and the in-patient psychotherapy unit at the Maudsley Hospital, NHS psychotherapy is no longer available in London for seriously disturbed patients requiring hospitalisation. The loss of such treatment units also means the disappearance of important training opportunities for the psychiatrists and psychologists to whom responsibility for accurate assessment of disturbed patients remains.

Three formal professional trainings – as a clinical psychologist and as a child and adult psychotherapist – have not in my opinion taught me as much about psychopathology as my years of 'apprenticeship' in the Shenley Psychotherapy Unit, under the supervision of Dr Leslie Sohn, and my gratitude to him is immense.

My experience with learning-disabled children came about by chance when I took up two clinical psychology sessions at a special children's unit in Brent. It was to be a temporary move and was intended merely to save the sessions till a suitably experienced psychologist could be recruited. A stay that was to be measured in months lasted five years. I was unprepared for all the discoveries I was to make there about autistic behaviour, expecting there to be little that I as a psychoanalytic psychologist could offer or learn in such a setting. For the many opportunities to learn about autism and learning disability which I found there, I am grateful to the children and staff of St Andrew's House. It was a privilege to be able to share thinking with teachers and staff there about the enormous burdens of containment required of them while they continued to shoulder that burden every day.

The Willesden Centre Workshop on Psychoanalytic Approaches to Learning Disability has grown from that experience. Clinical psychologists now applying psychoanalytic principles to management practices in such settings report encouraging results, particularly in relation to violent and disruptive behaviour. I am grateful to Asha Desai, Scott Galloway, Sue Hooper, Lucy Baxter, Koffi Krafona and other members of the Workshop for sharing their experiences and ideas, some of which I have quoted in the book.

This book is about internal processes and the development of capacities in humans to investigate the world they inhabit. In this task Bion drew attention to the order of the growth of knowledge, holding that knowledge of the psychical and the way humans construe their perceptions must precede knowledge of the physical world they perceive. The corollary in all psychoanalytic undertakings is the reason why the analysis of the practitioners is crucial. In my own internal investigations, I am indebted to Mrs Margaret Rustin and to Dr Murray Jackson, more than I can say.

My thanks also go to Laurence Spurling and to Edwina Welham whose experience and encouraging 'background presence' helped to keep me on task, and to Margaret Walker of the Tavistock Centre Library for her unstinting generosity of time.

Introduction

'Autistic' derives from the Greek *autos*, self, and was first used by Bleuler in his specification of the diagnostic features of schizophrenia (Bleuler 1911). He used the term then to describe the quality of withdrawal he had observed in schizophrenic patients who appeared to be absorbed exclusively in their own internal experience. Later, this description was also applied by Kanner to a group of children in whom he observed a common feature which he found striking (Kanner 1943). It was the shutting out or ignoring by the children of anything coming from outside them and their resulting state of extreme aloneness. By giving the name 'autism' to this phenomenon, the term was immediately associated exclusively with this particular diagnostic group, rather hijacking its use for further examination of the nature and incidence of the particular withdrawal behaviour which had been observed. The separation of autism and psychosis which resulted was probably premature, but the division which was established then is now being vigorously maintained and contributes in no small measure, I think, to the continuing confusions and controversies associated with the investigation of the origins of both conditions.

This book is not primarily a biography but is about the distinguished contribution to the psychoanalytic investigation of autism which Frances Tustin has made. She has been a controversial figure in this field and I think it is appropriate to be mindful of the considerable opposition within child psychiatry today to any idea based on looking at autism from a psychoanalytic perspective. In some quarters, the psychoanalytic treatment of autistic children can even be deemed unethical on the grounds that it might stimulate unrealistic expectations. Much of the opposition to a psychoanalytic approach to autism comes from misconceptions imposed on it by outsiders to psychoanalysis, basing their criticisms very often on out-of-date interpretations of Freud. Therapists are very familiar with the problem of being misunderstood. They are often having to defend themselves against the misattribution to them of ideas they do not hold and against accusations of being ignorant of ideas which in fact inform their work. I hope that this book will help towards a very necessary clarification of what has and has not been claimed.

Another oppositional force of great significance lies in the existence of powerful pressures to foreclose further thinking about the phenomena of autistic withdrawal by calling the condition biological. What is 'biological' seems to be understood as excluding the psychological as if the evolution of the psyche were a discrete development and did not belong within the continuity of biological and evolutionary development. I think this is a measure of the difficulties of thinking about so primitive a level of comprehending the world and of conceptualising the formative interface between sensation and thinking which brings the psyche into being.

Both Bion and Tustin, in their very different ways of expressing ideas about the origins of human thinking, emphasise the primitive, sensory and pre-verbal nature of the components of experience which go into the development of mentation. They share the view that the containment and management of primitive organismic anxiety is crucial to that development. Both consider that the experience of containment for the infant is in large part contingent on the availability of a receptive maternal object. This does not imply that mothers are responsible for their child's psychic development but that they play a significant part in what is indubitably a joint enterprise.

In this book I have been interested in the re-assessment of the tenuous links first observed between autism and psychosis, with the aim more of illuminating psychosis than autism. The understanding of borderline psychotic patients, for instance, may well be extended by the detection of hitherto unrecognised autistic levels of defence against existential terror. There are strong indications, too, that autistic terrors of dissolution and loss of existence underscore in obsessionality, the desperation to hold on to concrete reality. We have yet to discover, for example, whether it might be possible that the autistic child feels *he* does not exist when he is treating others as if *they* did not.

The seeming impenetrability of autism is a source of fascination and intellectual challenge for psychologists and all students of mind. Curiosity and the human drive towards understanding and finding meaning in the world has characterised humans since pre-history and it is their development of knowledge and imagination which differentiates them from all other animals. At the same time, this distinctive achievement deriving primarily from the sensory apparatus is firmly rooted in the biological make-up. Of the human senses, two, sight and hearing, dominate our outlook. Knowledge of the outside world comes mainly through the eyes whilst hearing gives access to the liveness of people and living creatures. Although other senses also come into play, the dominance and distinctiveness of vision as the means of gaining information about the world and sound as the means of gaining information about people in the world is significant and very relevant to the perplexities of autism.

The creative importance in the coming together of the seen object and the heard object is unmistakable when it first occurs in the baby's early cooing response to the attentive mother. The autistic child is distinctive in the apparent attempt to dispense with hearing so that deafness is often the parents' first conjecture. In both autistic and psychotic individuals a primary obstacle to treatment is the difficulty in engaging the patient in listening to the therapist. In autism the withdrawal is overt and uncompromising. In psychosis a much more subtle form of disconnection takes place where the patient hears but does not heed. One patient, as she began to become aware of this, put it quite graphically when she said, 'I hear you, but it doesn't go past my ears.'

The book has two objectives: first, to give an account of Tustin's clinical work and principal ideas, and secondly, to try to place her contribution within the tradition of psychoanalytic thinking and theory. To put autism into perspective, it seemed appropriate also to include an historical introduction to the nosology of the disturbances of childhood.

The first two chapters of this book are biographical and the material for this section was obtained largely from the reminiscences of Frances Tustin herself. We first met, professionally, when I visited her for supervision many years ago. Finding that we shared much in common in our thinking, we continued to meet and discuss ideas from time to time and a close and lasting friendship has developed. She has been hugely generous in entrusting me with original letters, clinical notes, manuscripts, photographs, all of which have furnished a vivid picture of her life and her career. Her friends and colleagues have also contributed in various ways to clarify and confirm facts or to fill gaps of memory. She has taken a close interest in the book and in the series.

Chapter 3 introduces Tustin's first book, published in 1972, in which she adumbrates her principal ideas on autism. It is presented in the context of the contemporaneous work on autism which was going on in America and in England to which she was indebted in formulating her own individual ideas. The influence of Mahler is strong but led her into conceptual difficulties which she later tried to remedy. Her debt to Meltzer and to Bick is implicit in her adaptation of 'adhesive identification' to produce the 'sensory' world which she saw as characterising autism, and her gratitude to both is explicit for their personal help in supervising her early work. She was a member, for a time, of Meltzer's Autism Workshop from which in 1975 another influential book on autism emerged.

Chapter 4 puts the discovery of autism into the historical context of the gradual and reluctant recognition of the existence of psychiatric disorder in children.

Chapter 5 describes and gives illustrations of Tustin's two major categories of autistic disorder, to which she gives the names 'encapsulated' and 'entangled'. The former coincides with the Kanner syndrome while the latter, a much more confusional state, might be classified by some as more schizophrenic-like than autistic. The differentiation of these two primitive states of mind has been particularly helpful to the understanding and management of learning-impaired children and this is discussed in detail in Chapter 11.

Chapter 6 deals with the most primitive existential fears which Tustin has related to the premature experience of bodily separateness from the mother.Tustin has described this ultimate trauma as a 'black hole' experience, using an image commonly found in the language of borderline and psychotic patients, who may even have concrete experiences of yawning chasms into which they might fall. Both she and Grotstein see the trauma of nothingness and meaninglessness as the most dreaded human experience. Psychosis, by creating an alternative world, is, therefore, the ultimate desperate defence against this black hole of autistic depression.

Tustin's emphasis on the significance for psychic development of body-centred modes of experience is taken up in Chapter 7. She believes that autism is the result of trauma which dissipates the sense of bodily containment. Since bodily containment is a necessary pre-requisite to psychic development, this prejudices mental growth. This chapter also outlines Ogden's expansion of these ideas to conceptualise an 'autistic-contiguous' position as the most primitive form of psychological organisation, operative from birth and pre-dating the paranoid-schizoid position.

Autistic objects, another of Tustin's important contributions, are discussed in Chapter 8. Autistic objects are of two types with distinct functions. They may be hard objects giving hard sensations to hold on to, or they may comprise soft sensations of the body or its products to blur the edges of separateness. These are differentiated from transitional objects which belong to the more integrated level of whole object experience.

Chapter 9 gives an account of Tustin's treatment of Peter, augmenting previously published excerpts with material from original notes. Some most interesting follow-up information about Peter's educational career is included, as well as observations of Peter, the young adult.

Chapters 10 and 11 discuss one of the most important areas to benefit from the application of Tustin's ideas and formulations, learning disability. Tustin's focus on the personality disruptions which can occur at a primitive inchoate, pre-thinking level has been highly relevant to learning impairment, long associated with early developmental failures. The significance of emotional containment to mental growth has also led to a new appreciation of the factors involved in adult conditions of learning difficulty. Where there is an autistic failure to engage with psychic life, the damage to learning potential is deep and results in intractable problems of dissatisfaction and failure to achieve. This chronic and severe autistic condition is frequently diagnosed as 'mild' learning difficulty because of the absence of psychotic symptomatology. Case illustrations in Chapter 10 demonstrate how difficulties that can be deemed mild seen from one vertex can from another reveal disjunctions of grave significance.

The delineation of her two constellations of autistic behaviour, which are commonly found among the learning-disabled, has been of direct help, especially in institutions, in finding ways of understanding bizarre meaningless or erratic behaviour. When the withdrawn, emotionally 'frozen' states or the confused and volatile states of entanglement are recognised and appreciated, domestic relationships and routines change. Understanding increases emotional containment in the carers and, where psychodynamically informed management is available in residential units, benefits are beginning to accrue.

In Chapter 12, I have looked briefly at mythology, as the earliest evidence of attempts to structure human experience. These pictorial accounts of an understanding of life, akin to the visualisations of dreaming, represent the emergence of a capacity for imagination and mark an achievement of great moment for the development of thought. Since this is the capacity which has been discovered to be significantly absent in autism, the condition becomes interesting in the context of evolutionary development. Lacking an 'inner eye', the autistic child relies heavily on the 'external' eye and confuses its function, fearful, like the obsessional, that people may enter or be entered through the eye. The absence of the inner life of imagination in autism, which has been experimentally demonstrated, may itself constitute the 'black hole' against which psychosis and obsessionality defend.

Chapter 1

Growing up in the bosom of the church

Frances Daisy Vickers was born in Darlington in the North of England on 15 October 1913 and her lifetime therefore spans two world wars. She was the only child of two deeply religious people, devoted to their work in the Church of England. Her mother had been trained as a church sister, at the prestigious Chelsea College in London, and outside the family she was always addressed as 'Sister Minnie'. What impressed the little Frances most was the long heliotrope dress and caped coat which her mother wore, the mark of her college training. The colour remains her favourite, to this day.

It was in the course of her pastoral work as a deaconess that Sister Minnie met the striking young man she was to marry. He had been trained in the Church Army as a Lay Reader, and was an impressive preacher. They shared an intense interest in religious life but came to differ violently about what that meant. Their different understandings of personal relationships and their approaches to the doubts and questions inevitably raised in the minds of intelligent people were diametrically opposed. She was accepting and compliant, a supplicant, while he was a radical and a non-conformist.

George Vickers was fourteen years younger than his bride and this is likely to have added to the difficulties the couple experienced in developing mutual understanding. Their first and only baby was born just before the outbreak of the First World War. She was named after her two aunts; Frances after her father's sister and Daisy after her mother's. For George, there was little time to adapt to becoming a father before he had to leave home to become an army chaplain. Frances was one year old when her father left for France. He was taken prisoner there and Frances was five before she was to see him again.

The first five years of her life were spent close to her mother in an atmosphere of smothering devotion to the Church's teaching. She was a good obedient little girl, the epitome of Emily Shapcote's idealised Child of God.

Make me Lord, obedient, mild
as becomes a little child
All day long, in every way
Teach me what to do and say.

Accepting all her mother's beliefs, she was a compliant child, more than satisfying all that was expected of her, but she was also able to sense the insecurity and the hidden terrors which lay beneath her mother's need for them both to be bright and shining candles, lighting a world of 'darkness and sin'. An enthusiastic member of the Band of Hope, however, Frances was ever confident that she was indeed a 'sunbeam for Jesus'.

Mother embraced her baby with a devotion that was as fierce as that with which she clung to the Church. The result, not surprisingly, was that the little girl very early began to be filled with a sense of great responsibility and importance but she also grew to believe that her mother's need was so great that it seemed it was the daughter who was doing the parenting. One touching memory of this is of the four-year-old Frances feeling that she could guide her mother in the black-out, because she was nearer the pavement and so could see the steps better. Brought up, in many ways, to be a little 'sister', she may have perceived her mother as more of a worried big sister than a mother.

It would not have been easy for George Vickers to secure a place again in this family, either as a father or as a husband, where mother and daughter had become so united and where there was also a wife who felt she was wedded as much to the Church as to her husband. To this obstacle was added the change which had overtaken his beliefs and his outlook on life during his sojourn as a prisoner of war. When he did return, he had lost the faith to which his wife so resolutely adhered, having become deeply disillusioned by the Church's attitudes to war. He became a pacifist and a socialist and, on leaving the army, he took the family to Sheffield where Frances began her school life and Father started to study at the university to begin a new career as a teacher.

For the next ten years, Frances was caught in the desperate and sometimes bitter conflict which developed between her parents. Her first five years had been spent close to Mother in an atmosphere of unquestioning devotion and obedience to the Church. Now, all her mother's teaching came under the fire of her father's criticism. The devout deaconess began to fear that her husband had been contaminated by the devil. Contemporary authors and thinkers, like Shaw and Freud and the progressive educationist A.S. Neill, who so fascinated her husband, were considered by Sister Minnie to be wicked and evil.

Remnants of nineteenth-century anarchism, which continued to interest left-wing thinkers after the war and underpinned Neill's ideas on education, held a compelling attraction for George Vickers, too. Like many others of his generation, he was a young man who became ensnared in a tangle of confusion and personal conflict as a result of his wartime experiences. His sudden exposure on the battlefield to the primitive conditions of life in the raw challenged his acceptance of all the traditionally held beliefs of his religion and training. An internal struggle for reconciliation of his thoughts and beliefs was mirrored in the turbulent conflicts with his conservative wife about beliefs and truths. It was a struggle about allowing thinking and it was a conflict to which an intelligent daughter, caught in the middle, could not be immune.

Frances's memories of her mother are now coloured with sadness and regret that she could not then appreciate the positive qualities in her attitudes and beliefs. Her own emotional need to separate herself from her mother's influence led her to collude with her father's criticisms and she began to feel contempt for the simplicity and naivety of her mother's thinking. Her own education and her admiration for her father made it increasingly difficult for her to see how she could give a place to her mother's point of view. Instead, she began to see her mother's ideas as silly and snobbish and joined with her father in considering her narrow-minded and superstitious. Quite apart from the oedipal dynamic, Father was attractive because he was more fun and he had a strong sense of humour. It was unfortunate that his humour could, at times, be at Mother's expense.

In due course, after completion of his training, her father was attracted to country schools and soon became the headmaster of a village school, which meant that Frances became one of his pupils. This now bestowed the rather special place in her father's world that she had previously enjoyed in the earlier days with her mother, in the Band of Hope. As the daughter of the headmaster, she enjoyed the new playground status, and, like her father, she also loved living in the country. If father and daughter were happy about this change of environment, however, mother was not. She much preferred the cultural life of the town which she saw as superior but she was also timid and felt uncomfortable in the country, afraid of cows, dogs and the dark.

She disapproved of her husband's informality, as much as she did his socialist views. Differences became concretised with Mother disapproving of Father's cloth cap, whilst he was contemptuous of her penchant for white evening gloves. She loved the theatre, he loved Nature. In the North, Mother had felt she had to protect her London refinements and educate her daughter according to the standards of her own upbringing. Father, on the other hand, was a Lincolnshire man, of farming stock, a man of the people; all the same, equally proud of his forebears. He would often impress his daughter with stories about their connections with outstanding religious leaders of the past. His family had been connected with the Quaker movement and he counted Elizabeth Fry, the prison reformer, among his ancestors. He also included Sarah Crisp, a follower of John Wesley, who, he emphasised, had been the first woman preacher. It was not lost on the young Frances even then that women could achieve great things; at that time she was bent on becoming a naturalist.

Frances remembers visiting Summerhill, the progressive school founded by A.S. Neill in 1921 in a Suffolk village. She and her father stayed there for a week and she thinks he might well have taken a post at the school but for her mother's intense opposition to Neill and his associates. Neill was reputed to have been analysed by Wilhelm Reich and such activities were condemned by her mother as sinful.

It would seem to have been a lonely life for a little girl, although Frances appears mostly to remember the activity and the earnestness of their lives. Besides, she had always felt herself to be a focus of interest and attention. She was at the centre of her mother's life and work, she was a leading light among her peers in the Band of Hope and, as the daughter of the headmaster, she enjoyed centre stage once again. A serious-minded child, she nevertheless enjoyed her popularity. It was not undeserved, for she was cheerful, intelligent and kind, and popularity may also have helped to fill many a gap in her childhood experience. The ease with which she could make friends has lasted throughout her life.

Life was unsettling not only as a result of the parental controversies, but also because of the many removals of her home as they followed Father's career changes. She remembers a brief period of living in Scotland at the end of the war, before she went to school and before they returned to Sheffield. After Sheffield came her father's moves to different schools in Lincolnshire. Her life must have been full of lost friendships but in retrospect Frances sees all these uprootings as having produced a certain adaptability in her.

When Frances won a scholarship to Sleaford High School at age twelve, they lived so far from a station that she had to become a boarder.

She had always loved school and she found the cooler intellectual atmosphere of boarding school a welcome relief from the hotbed of controversy at home. Her enjoyment of boarding school was later to cause some surprise in John Bowlby when he came to be interviewing her for the child psychotherapy training course at the Tavistock Clinic.

One year after her admission to Sleaford, she had to change school again, when her father moved to a different country school, this time within reach of a railway station so that Frances could become a day girl again. She transferred to Grantham High School, an institution now distinguished by another of its former pupils, Margaret Thatcher. It was while she was at this school, thirteen years old and doing well enough to be in the scholarship stream, with her sights on Oxford, that her mother took the momentous decision that they must leave her father. Had Frances stayed at Grantham, it seems likely that she would have gone on to university to study biology, her favourite subject.

It must have been a touching scene as she and her mother and a big black trunk waited in a country lane for the bus to come and take them to a new life. Perhaps her mother thought she was protecting her daughter from the unconventional anarchic and 'sinful' views of her father; perhaps she thought she was bringing her back to the civilising influences of the town. What it was that finally proved the last straw in the marriage, no one knows. For Frances, the separation came as a complete shock. It was a severance from all that she most valued: her love of the countryside, which she shared with her father, her school and the hopes of achievements there and, above all, her father whom she did admire and love despite his faults. For a moment, she even wondered helplessly whether there was somewhere to hide, so as not to be torn away in this unceremonious manner. Such a sudden enforced rift with her father was too much to bear and in the interests of soldiering on, and in characteristic fashion, of putting her best foot forward, she quietly supported her mother; during this period of her life, denial was her mainstay. She was seen and saw herself as a confident, cheerful and 'balanced' personality but the real impact of this momentous experience was to remain encapsulated and concealed from her, until her analysis with Bion, many years later.

Whatever her mother had in her mind, the outcome was that they travelled round England for a whole year, living with friends and relatives before her mother finally returned to Sheffield to work in a small, rather run-down church. Here they were as poor as the proverbial church mice. In this 'home' the intellectual atmosphere was stifled by a Christianity which was narrow, concrete and felt close to superstition, but they were back in town and Frances could go to school again. Her scholarship was transferred and she resumed her education at a teacher-training school in Sheffield. When she finally passed matriculation, it was decided that she should go on to a teacher-training college rather than to university, to save on time and money.

Financial constraints would no doubt have been of prime importance, but Frances's mother probably also had in mind the strong presence of the church at Whitelands, the chosen High Anglican college in London. Mother would have been reassured in entrusting her daughter to the Whitelands environment rather than to the more open air of a university where she might have encountered some of her father's ideas. All the same, I think that the canny Frances also saw in the teacher training a quicker route to professional and financial independence and freedom from the influence of her mother.

Chapter 2

Professional development

In 1932 Frances Vickers entered Whitelands Church of England College and it was to prove one of the formative influences in her life. One of the earliest colleges for the training of women teachers, it had a most distinguished history. Its foundation had been supported by Charles Dickens and John Ruskin. The latter took a close personal interest in the life of the college and gave gifts of hundreds of books and pictures. The college had just moved from Chelsea to Putney by the time Frances arrived there. Among the art treasures brought from the college's Chelsea home to Whitelands were thirteen stained-glass windows by Edward Burne-Jones. The beauty of the college interiors greatly impressed the country girl; the chapel and its windows especially. Its ambience of peace proffered a safe haven at a key time after the rough passage of her childhood home and she still thinks of her stay there as a healing experience.

Not immune to the intellectual controversies of the time, the college took a keen interest in contemporary thinking in all that pertained to education, but its debates were conducted in a spirit of generosity and tolerance that was a revelation to Frances. The quiet benevolent atmosphere of the college and the openness and tolerance of the Christian teaching there were a relief and a pleasure to one who had been torn between the relentless dialectics of her father's thinking and the imprisoning rigidities of her mother's beliefs. She found herself much at ease there and remembers with tenderness the evening service, the Office of Compline – 'I shall repose upon thy eternal changelessness . . . '

There was much to excite the curiosity of the newcomer. The college had taken a keen interest in the new psychology which was beginning to sweep through education in the early twentieth century. The ideas of Homer Lane, the pioneering and controversial educationist, had an unequivocal place in the college curriculum. Lane was one of the first to introduce psychological principles into the education and reform of delinquent children in his experimental reformatory called The Little Commonwealth.

Tucked away in the Dorsetshire hills, Lane attempted to demonstrate the success of a regime based on re-education rather than constraint and punishment. It was a regime founded on his three principles of Love, Freedom and Self-Government, principles which he believed to be universally applicable. For those with an interest in the new ideas of psychology, Lane was an inspiring teacher and therapist, but to conventional and conservative minds, he was a menace, his attitudes and ideas deeply suspect.

Following allegations of sexual misconduct made against him by one of his own pupils, Lane was brought to trial in 1924. It was an early hint of the psychotic entanglements that nowadays would quickly attract the label 'sexual abuse'. Such perceptual distortions characteristic of psychosis will be discussed below (see Chapters 5 and 10). At the trial, Winifred Mercier, Principal of Whitelands, and much admired by Frances, had been one of those who spoke out in Lane's defence.

Frances was a promising student and showed, like her father, a natural talent for teaching. Biology continued to be a favourite subject at college but when she completed her training she chose to teach latency children of seven to nine years old. On graduating from the college, she returned to Sheffield to work, in order to be near to her mother who was, by then, in failing health. Like her father, but contrary to her mother's inclinations, she also became a socialist, and it was in the Sheffield Labour Party that she met her first husband, John Taylor, whom she married in 1938, just before the outbreak of the Second World War.

John was a Town Hall official and with Frances's teacher's salary they were able to afford to set up home together in a pleasant leafy suburb of Sheffield. Married life in her new home was not destined to last very long, however. They had a year there together, before her husband was called up into the forces, at the beginning of the war, and for most of the next five years their lives were spent apart, strikingly repeating the earlier pattern of her experience with her father.

Sister Minnie died in 1942 and it was then, after her mother's death, that Frances felt free to make a life of her own. Her husband abroad, she left Sheffield and returned to the South to take up a post in a progressive boarding school in Kent from where she was able to travel up to London in the evenings, to attend the Child Development Course run by Susan Isaacs at London University. It was at that time, too, that she became a member of Commonwealth, a liberal Christian group led by Sir Richard Ackland which filled an intellectual gap during the political coalition of the war years. Among the members of this group whom she met at that time was Arnold Tustin, the man who was later to become her second husband.

With the ending of the Second World War in 1945, conscripted soldiers everywhere were trying to restore their disrupted family and marital lives. When John and Frances came together again they found, like many others, that they had grown too far apart in the interim. Besides, Frances's professional and intellectual development in London had become too important for her to give up and return to Sheffield.

The couple finally decided to separate and the marriage later ended in divorce. It was an unhappy time for Frances but one which coincided with the re-emergence in her life of the reassuring influence of Whitelands. In 1946, although by this time an agnostic, she returned there to become a lecturer in education.

Two years later she married Arnold Tustin and soon after that, when he was appointed to the Chair of Electrical Engineering at Birmingham University, she left Whitelands and taught at Dudley Teachers' Training College, near Birmingham.

It was about this time too that she made contact again with her father. This came about, quite fortuitously, when she saw a letter of his in *The Times* newspaper and wrote to him at the address given. She discovered that he now lived with another partner, Gladys. He had not divorced her mother and the couple did not marry until after Mrs Vickers's death.

Frances kept close contact with them both until their deaths. She got on well with Gladys and frequently went to stay with them. In that time she was to see again in her father's relationship with Gladys indications of the contempt with which he had treated her mother. She came to the conclusion that he held a low opinion of women in general and this confirmed her early conviction that he had not taken her education seriously, because, she thought, he did not see education as a proper province for women. He would often remind his daughter that the soul was more important than the intellect and that there were more important things in life than passing exams.

Frances spent a great deal of time with the couple as they grew older and she tended Gladys in her final illness till she died. The story of George Vickers's religious convictions took a final twist as he neared the end of his life, still deeply tortured by religious doubts. He became convinced that the Roman Catholic Church was the true path to salvation and he died a convert. Frances now comments wryly on his final return to the bosom of the Church, that the cunning old anarchist was 'hedging his bets'!

CHILD PSYCHOTHERAPY TRAINING

In 1949, tragedy struck Frances's second marriage when she lost their first baby through toxaemia of pregnancy. The following year, with Arnold's support, she turned her grief and disappointment into constructive endeavour and began to train as a child psychotherapist at the Tavistock Clinic, in London. Despite considerable logistical difficulties at the time, she began to immerse herself in the study of child psychology which was to occupy her for the rest of her life.

It was in 1950 that she became one of the first child psychotherapists to train at the Tavistock Clinic, joining the new Training Course for Non-Medical Child Psychotherapists which had been opened there in 1948. She commuted weekly from Birmingham to do so. Her contemporaries on the training course, the second ever, were Martha Harris, Dina Rosenbluth and Yvonne Haupt. Yvonne returned to her native South Africa on completion of the training, but the other three remained close friends for the rest of their lives. Frances has particularly fond memories of Martha Harris, whose kindness and generosity helped Frances so much during her training. Martha shared her home with Frances when she was hard-up and in need of somewhere to live for the week-days spent in London.

At the Tavistock Clinic, then situated in central London, close to Harley Street, she found two formidable teachers in John Bowlby and Esther Bick. John Bowlby, who interviewed her for the training vacancy, had been largely instrumental in bringing the training in child psychotherapy into being. At the time, there was considerable opposition within psychiatry to the idea of allowing non-medical professionals into therapeutic contact with psychologically disturbed children. It was with Bowlby's vigorous support that the training course for child psychotherapists finally succeeded in gaining recognition but the profession was to carry the designation 'non-medical'. The ambivalence of this title remained for many years and it was not until 1972 that the 'non-medical' prefix could be dropped and the profession was able to feel fully accepted. The first doctor to join the training course arrived in 1975.

John Bowlby, a researcher as well as a psychoanalyst, impressed Frances with his thoughtful and scholarly approach to psychotherapy. Notwithstanding his Scottish origins, she sums up her own lasting impression of him as 'a top-drawer Englishman'. Esther Bick, on the other hand, a passionate Polish refugee, created a very different impression and Frances was at first filled with misgivings about the fervour of her support for Mrs Klein and her work. In time, she came to appreciate Mrs Bick's clinical acuity and found her an inspiring teacher.

Mrs Bick gave precedence to the infant's internal world of phantasy, while Bowlby studied the external evidence of the quality of the infant's attachment to the caregiver. The problem of discriminating between these internal and external factors in child development and of preserving both the distinctions between the two and their complementarity continues to present as many difficulties today as it did then. The controversy between Bick and Bowlby finally resulted in Bick's leaving the Tavistock Clinic, although she continued to be a leading influence in the Child Psychotherapy Group as an external teacher and supervisor.

Mrs Bick had first experienced baby observation in Vienna where she studied child psychology under Charlotte Buhler. Convinced of the value of baby observation, she was, however, determined to adopt a very different methodology from that which she had learned in the Psychology Department of the University of Vienna. There the stop-watch had reigned and the stop-watch had no place in Mrs Bick's approach to observation. Her focus was on studying the emotional developments of infancy and their configurations, seeking to find evidence of internal structuralisations as they were coming into place. There are certain pitfalls associated with an investigative approach relying so heavily on subjective judgement and great scientific care needs to be exercised. I shall return to this important subject in other contexts later in this book.

Mrs Bick's method of observation of babies held a central place in the Tavistock child psychotherapy training from its inception and Frances has always felt particularly indebted to this aspect of her training. In 1962, baby observation was included in the training programme of the British Psychoanalytic Society and its importance is now widely recognised by training courses in psychoanalysis and psychoanalytic psychotherapy (adult and child) throughout the world.

It is a method of close observation of the baby for an hour at a time, free from concurrent recording of any kind, but written up in minute detail at the end of the observation. In their book *Closely Observed Infants* (Miller *et al.* 1989) the writers give a comprehensive account of the development and rationale of this method of study of infant mental development. Their discussion of the observation material also conveys the care and economy which needs to be exercised in the drawing of conclusions from such material.

It was Mrs Bick who was responsible for the choice of Tustin's training analyst. In 1950 she herself saw no reason to have an analysis at all, seeing herself (as indeed did others) as a well-balanced, sensitive and insightful woman. Her interest was in children, not in herself, she thought, but she accepted the analysis as a necessary but inconvenient part of the training. Wilfred Bion was unknown to her at that time and her recollection is of following Mrs Bick's instructions and of doing what she was told, in the interests of being a good trainee.

In her first encounter with Bion, she felt a strong dislike of him, finding him a frightening and forbidding figure. 'I thought, "This is terrible". The great bushy eyebrows and those stern eyes. I wondered what I'd come to. It felt as if he just took me and flung me on the couch. I was really quite frightened by him, I think. There were a lot of silences which I always hated' (personal communication). At the time, Frances talked freely to colleagues about her analysis and her ambivalence is illustrated by their recall of how she talked of challenging Bion at first by insisting on the merits of keeping your feet on the ground!

Contrary to her initial attitude to psychoanalysis, Frances was to remain in analysis with Bion for fourteen years (with two breaks, for an illness and her absence in the USA). Later, she was to have a very different experience of the man, remarking many times on the deep kindness which always accompanied his unwavering adherence to the truth.

Her three-year training in child psychotherapy at the Tavistock Clinic remains for her the cornerstone of her further development. Feeling greatly indebted to Esther Bick and John Bowlby, she began to make full use of what she had learned from them but, like her father, she retained a healthy scepticism and was ever alert to new problems and the questions which appeared to remain unanswered.

The first of these challenges came in 1952, following a talk given at the Clinic by Marion Putnam. Nine years after the publication of Kanner's first paper on autism (Kanner 1943), interest in the subject was gathering momentum, particularly in America, and Bowlby had taken an opportunity to invite Marion Putnam to come and speak about the work which was taking place at the James Jackson Putnam Research and Treatment Center in Boston. There, a special unit had been set up to study the needs of autistic children and their parents and families.

It was Marion Putnam, therefore, who first fired Tustin's interest in autism and introduced a whole new world of thinking about infant development and its adversities. Autism, at that time, seemed to be beyond the reach of Kleinian child psychotherapy, based as it was on the analysis of relationships and phantasied relationships; a considerable theoretical gap was encountered by psychotherapists in the face of the phenomena of autism. Tustin wasn't the only one whose interest was stimulated by the discovery of a new and deeper level of pathology. At the Tavistock Clinic, Bick had been working for many years with a deeply disturbed child whom she saw as schizophrenic (Bick 1968). In the 1950s, Popper and Bowlby were also interested in the new theoretical questions raised by the discovery of autism. Others at the Tavistock were to follow this interest, principal among them Hoxter (1972) and Bremner, Weddell, and Wittenberg. In the course of their work with psychotically disturbed children, they began to recognise the autistic features inherent in very early childhood disturbances. This work was later co-ordinated by Meltzer and published under his editorship (Meltzer *et al.* 1975).

The autistic child, unresponsive, unco-operative and uncommunicative, presented an immediate technical and theoretical problem. Discussing her own encounter with such a child (Klein 1930), Mrs Klein recognised the theoretical difficulties and, unable to commit herself to a diagnosis, concluded that the child, Dick, was suffering from 'an inhibition in development and not a regression'. She speculated that it was an excess of destructive violence in the early oral sadistic phase of mental development which overwhelmed all sources of libidinal pleasure and constituted the fixation point of schizophrenia. While she inclined to categorise Dick as schizophrenic, she was also well aware of inherent inconsistencies in making such a diagnosis but concluded that the evidence that would remove the theoretical and taxonomic problems still remained to be brought together.

The Putnam Center favoured a regime which combined Freudian ideas with a modification of behavioural methods of treatment and attempted to train autistic children to behave in more socially acceptable ways. It was an important learning experience for Tustin when she had the opportunity to spend a year there at the end of her Tavistock training. In her opinion, their techniques were not very well suited to the children's disturbances but the centre was innovative and lively and she made many friends among the staff there.

Contemporaneously, in the United States, a psychoanalytic approach to treatment was being developed by Bruno Bettelheim, at the University of Chicago. There, at his Orthogenic School for the treatment of autistic and psychotic children, treatment was based on Bettelheim's understanding of autism as a catastrophic withdrawal from life at a critical point, before the child has discovered his essential humanity. His ideas, first published in *The Empty Fortress* (1967), hold much in common with Bion and Tustin.

Chance, intuition and a capacity to recognise and seize opportunities have combined to further Tustin's work. At the end of her training, one such opportunity arose when Arnold Tustin was invited in 1954 to spend a year as visiting Webster Professor at MIT Cambridge, Massachusetts, not far therefore from Boston and the Putnam Center.

Encouraged and recommended by John Bowlby, Frances was able to take up an honorary appointment at the centre and for that year immersed herself in the daily lives of autistic children and their parents. It was a first-hand experience of primitive life in the raw, as she attempted to make some sense of the strange and outrageous behaviour of the children whom she had first heard about when she listened to Marion Putnam's paper.

Neither medically trained nor a psychologist, she was only allowed to participate in the therapeutic programme at the centre on the strength of her Tavistock training. There was, in addition, the respite care scheme offered to parents and this was of equal, if not greater, interest. Frances grasped this opportunity to go and live in the homes of autistic children, to look after them full-time, while their parents had a break. This provided an important new perspective and left Frances with a lasting respect for the burden placed on the parents of an autistic child.

Kanner's early speculations about the personalities of the parents of autistic children led to studies which fostered the notion of emotional coldness as a causative factor in autism and gave rise to the term 'refrigerator mother' (Kanner 1959, Eisenberg 1956, Creak and Ini 1960). Frances saw this as hurtful and unfair to the mothers whom she had personally come to know and she was strongly drawn to their defence. Sensitive to their plight, as she had once been to that of her own mother whom she saw as suffering at the hands of a callous husband, she was this time without ambivalence and her support and sympathy for the mothers of autistic children have been unstinting.

Autism and Childhood Psychosis (1972), her first book, was written at a critical period in Tustin's life when her relationships were in turmoil. She had left her analyst; she had left the Tavistock Child Guidance Centre; she had left the Workshop which Meltzer had set up for the study of autism; and she had moved out of London. She had also left behind her child-bearing years and she was carrying the pain and disappointment of losing the possibility of giving birth to a healthy child. (At the age of forty-two, she had lost a second baby through toxaemia of pregnancy.) It was now imperative that she find fulfilment in an affirmation of her creativity. Her mind bubbling with ideas, she felt driven to find satisfaction and relief in the writing of this book.

Chapter 3

The discovery of autism and the search to understand it

Ere time and place were, time and place were not,
When primitive Nothing, something straight begot
Then all proceeded from the great united What.

John Wilmot, Earl of Rochester (1647–80)

Prior to the publication of Leo Kanner's seminal paper in 1943, children and adults with autism were usually consigned to institutions for the 'feeble-minded'. They were not distinguished from others suffering from a range of conditions in which the common and prominent feature was the failure to develop normal personal relationships and the failure to learn. All such children were designated mentally deficient and ineducable and custodial care for life had long been considered to be the best that could appropriately be provided.

Kanner's paper was a study of a group of eleven children whom he was able to identify as manifesting 'essential common characteristics, to such an extent that they cannot but be considered as fundamentally alike, from the point of view of psychopathology'. Most of the children had been brought to his institution in Baltimore with the assumption that they were feeble-minded and their low scores on psychometric testing seemed to confirm this.

After careful examination, however, Kanner concluded that the children's cognitive potential was being obscured by a 'basic affective disorder' and that the common denominator in all the children was their 'disability to relate themselves in the ordinary way to people and situations from the beginning of life' (Kanner 1943). He laid great stress on what he called their 'autistic aloneness', thus introducing the possibility of an emotionally determined causation into mental impairment, a field in which an organic aetiology had hitherto been considered axiomatic.

An original and controversial paper, which instantly brought closer together the frontiers of mental illness and mental deficiency, it stimulated great interest and opened a debate about the nature of autism and its aetiology which has continued ever since. The understanding of autistic phenomena now occupies an important position in the psychological and philosophical search to understand the nature and origins of mind. In this quest, the issue that remains outstanding and unresolved is the function and significance of affect in early mental development.

COGNITIVE DEFICIT

Much of the psychological research which followed Kanner's hypothesis about the significance of affect emphasised instead the cognitive deficit in autism.This was in line with the contemporary development of child psychiatry and its converse interest, in drawing attention to the role of intellectual impairment and organic brain damage in the aetiology of infantile psychosis. Cameron (1955, 1958) even sought to establish that intellectual impairments could play a crucial part in originating the psychotic process.

The empirical research which followed Kanner's paper increasingly paid attention to the identification of the qualities of the cognitive impairment indisputably present in autism (Hermelin and O'Connor 1970, Rutter and Schopler 1978, Rutter 1979, De Meyer *et al.* 1971). By the mid-1980s, Rutter, summing up the cumulative research evidence (Rutter 1983,1985), was drawing the conclusion that cognitive deficit was fundamental to autism and an integral part of the condition, underlying all other features, including the 'affective disorder' identified by Kanner. He saw this deficit as a cognitive inability rather than a disturbance of cognitive functioning, postulating an impairment of brain capacities, not necessarily involving organic pathology or brain disease. His conception of a specific, intrinsic impairment of brain *capacities* set a biological seal on autism which implicitly, and later explicitly, discouraged further research interest into affective psychogenic factors (Gillberg 1988, 1990, Steffenberg and Gillberg 1990), leaving considerations in that arena to the psychoanalysts.

THE PSYCHODYNAMIC APPROACH

Pre-eminent among the psychoanalysts with an interest in pursuing Kanner's findings from the 1950s onwards were Margaret Mahler in New York, Bruno Bettelheim at the University of Chicago and Donald

Meltzer in London. Influenced by all three, Frances Tustin, a child psychotherapist, published her first book on childhood autism in 1972. Hers was also a psychoanalytic view and it was both eclectic and individual.

Her first book was called *Autism and Childhood Psychosis* and it was the culmination of twenty years' experience of working with disturbed children. She has since had regrets about the title which, she fears, may have implied for some that she did not consider autistic children to be psychotic. A better title, she has suggested (Tustin 1981), would have been The Autism *of* Childhood Psychosis. Tustin's psychoanalytic interest in investigating the connections between the two conditions – a feature of her first book – was paralleled in the field of psychiatric research by a number of investigations of possible links between autism and schizophrenia (Hermelin and O'Connor 1970).

It was not until the 1980s that psychoanalytic theory and research methodology began to be brought together (Fraiberg 1982, Fonagy *et al.* 1991a, 1991b) and Hobson began his work on applying a research method to psychodynamic theories of autism (Hobson 1984, 1985, 1986).

AUTISM AND PSYCHOSIS

By 1979 it had been clearly established that there were distinct differences of pathology between autism and psychosis and that autism was not a form of early onset schizophrenia (Wolff and Barlow 1979). Following their Camberwell Survey (Wing and Gould 1979), Wing established her triad of autistic symptoms (impairment of social interaction, impairment of social communication and impairment of imaginative development) by broadening Kanner's criteria for autism to include psychotic children manifesting some autistic 'features'. Kanner's 'severe autistic aloneness', a critical feature of his syndrome, which referred to his perception of the state of mind of the autistic child, she equated with social isolation. This subtle change of emphasis is disregarded by Wing. To the psychodynamic psychologist, however, it brings about a significant shift of focus on the determining criteria from the intra-personal to the inter-personal field.

Wing proposed a continuum of autistic disturbance (Wing 1988) and it was then but a short step to subsume in this spectrum the categories of childhood psychosis as specified in the International Classification of Diseases (ICD-9). Finally, as it was argued by Gillberg (1990), all autistic and psychotic disorders of childhood could be included within the group

Pervasive Developmental Disorder as specified in the Diagnostic and Statistical Manual (DSM-IIIR). Wing's objective of diagnostic clarification and simplification rests on a critical and barely acknowledged redefinition of Kanner's criteria. It has encouraged erosion of distinctions in symptomatology and discouraged specificity. Alvarez, in a review of the controversies about autism, remarks: 'What the child is *not* may be taking precedence over what he *is*' (Alvarez 1992).

THE TUSTIN PERSPECTIVE

Tustin's understanding of early childhood autism is presented in an imaginative and individual style. She has learned a great deal from the children she has treated but, like Klein, she also draws on personal insights gained from her own life experiences. Her indebtedness to her psychoanalyst, Wilfred Bion, is something which continued to grow long after the analysis ended. His influence undoubtedly contributed to her way of thinking about autism but this has often been more apparent to others than to Tustin herself. A comment attributed to the late Oliver Lyth was that she seemed to have absorbed from the atmosphere of the couch what the rest of us have to learn from reading and re-reading his books. Be that as it may, Tustin is the first to acknowledge the difficulties she has in understanding much of what Bion writes.

Her first work was a courageous attempt to enter the inhospitable, mindless and pre-verbal world of the autistic child. In it, Tustin presented an account of her clinical work and the constructions and formulations she had arrived at in the course of her extensive clinical experience and her personal acquaintance with many autistic children and their families.

She wrote with honesty and an enthusiasm to bring this *terra incognita* into the light of understanding and communicability. To the Kleinian terminology of her training, she enlisted concepts from Mahler, Bettelheim and Winnicott and tried to bestow some scientific objectivity by welding the whole into a classificatory system. The attempt was premature and the book, loosely held together round her clinical studies, had a severely divided reception. In some quarters it was welcomed with acclaim, in others it was dismissed as an outrage to credibility and science.

James Anthony, Professor of Child Psychiatry at Washington University, in a lengthy review attempting to address the divergent impact of the book, entitled his article 'Tustin in Kleinianland' (Anthony 1973) and in it parodies Lewis Carroll's Alice: 'I almost wish

I hadn't read this book and gone down the "black hole" of Kleinian interpretation – and yet – and yet – it's rather curious you know, this sort of metapsychological life.' He is respectful of Tustin's honesty, but sceptical of her science, drawing attention with benevolence and good humour to places in the book where fantasy is mistaken for fact. It is a tribute to Tustin's integrity that she did not lose the courage of her convictions but was spurred on to re-examine the foundations of her formulations and to apply a greater rigour to her thinking. In subsequent books she reworks and expands on her ideas, most of which are adumbrated in this first book.

She has always relied more on evoking 'resonances' in her readers than on offering hard scientific evidence for her views but this is in part a function of the difficult terrain she is trying to chart. Wilfred Bion also noted the scientific problem intrinsic to all psychoanalytic investigation: how to communicate to others in the absence (for them) of the phenomena upon which understandings had been reached (Bion 1967). Nevertheless, her intuitive understandings do find recognition and her work is valued by clinicians world-wide.

Her hunch that her views are more readily acceptable in Roman Catholic countries she puts down to their cultural familiarity with the concept of soul and its protection from evil. For Tustin, the autistic seems to inhabit a godless world, in which the autistic shell is the last refuge, and this has echoes of Bettelheim's Empty Fortress, the ultimate protection from a hell that is inescapable (Bettelheim 1967).

She sees Early Infantile Autism as a pathological barrier created by fixation at a sensation-dominated, pre-thinking stage of infantile psychological development. It is an arrest rather than a regression. She believes that 'the stoppage of and the deviation from on-going psychological development has arisen as the result of the shock of traumatic awareness in infancy of bodily separateness from the mothering person' (Tustin 1972). In other words, the experience of separatedness has been premature and traumatic and the autistic withdrawal is the ultimate defence against psychotic depression. The 'black hole' of psychotic depression is a state in which the predominant fear is of annihilation of the sense of self or of 'falling for ever' as Winnicott expressed it (Winnicott 1958).

NORMAL AUTISM

It was unfortunate that Tustin chose to follow Mahler in calling this early psychologically formative stage of human development 'autistic' for she never wholly subscribed to it in her own thinking, despite her paper in 1991 'revising' her views. Mahler's position was coloured by her acceptance of the traditional Freudian view of infant development based on Freud's notion of a stimulus 'barrier', needed to protect the neonate from an excess of stimulation in the first few weeks of life (Freud 1920). Freud's stimulus barrier, albeit a concept arrived at through complex scientific and biological arguments, fitted well with Mahler's speculations about a pseudo-uterine period of mental development. This concept still remains useful in considering pathological experience although subsequent research evidence led Mahler to withdraw her use of the term 'normal autism' (Mahler 1985). Her substitution of a period of 'awakening' was close to Stern's 'emergence' (Stern 1985) and seems closer to the way in which Tustin had always conceptualised what she called 'normal' autism.

It was a serious mistake to use the same term for both a normal and a pathological condition, but this has perpetuated confusion rather than amplified error. For example, it would be both bizarre and erroneous to speak of the infant's early physical unco-ordination as 'normal cerebral palsy' but the intended comparison would be recognisable at a certain, not very useful, level.

It has certainly not been useful to refer to the first stages of infant psychological development as normal autism but Tustin does not use the term in the Mahler sense. Even in her first book, she talks of 'an innate disposition to recognise patterns, repetitions and continuities' and of the 'complexity and delicacy of the time-consuming process of becoming aware of the world and its objects, persons and other minds'. In a later paper in which she discusses her thinking about autistic 'shapes' and what she calls 'innate forms' (Tustin 1984a) she arrives at conclusions about the significance and function of shapes in psychic development which closely resemble the findings of the developmentalists (Bower 1971, Meltzoff and Moore 1977, Meltzoff 1981). In seeing shapes as 'the primary moulds in which the early experience was cast' (Tustin 1986) is she not expressing in her own imaginative way that 'the infant from the earliest days of life, forms and acts upon abstract representations of qualities of perception' (Stern 1985)?

In her struggle to understand the autistic condition, Tustin borrowed freely from science and from literature, wherever she found a term or an image which helped to portray her own concept of autism. Her enthusiasm to find the creative idea sometimes led her into inaccuracies and perhaps she could be accused of 'making things mean what she wants them to mean' (Carroll 1871). All the same, what she means by autism is not a stimulus-awaiting state of passivity but a primitively active pre-thinking existence which, under adverse conditions, can become ossified into an anti-thinking mode (Tustin 1972).

For this pre-thinking stage of mental development, autism is a misnomer. Tustin, like Meltzer (Meltzer *et al.* 1975), emphasises the predominantly sensory, proto-mental world of the autistic child, where sensation-engendered activity has been invested with a protective function. The importance they both ascribe to sensory activity is consistent with modern infant research findings in which the sensory modalities have been found to play a significant role in early mental organisation and the organising process itself is experienced by the infant as an 'emerging sense of self' (Escalona 1953, Stern 1985). What Tustin could not have adduced retrospectively and pathomorphically was the infant's intrinsic interest in social relatedness, for this is what has been lost or broken in autism.

The newest and most exciting development in infant research is, I think, the finding that babies have an innate capacity to recognise correspondences across the perceptual modalities. The medium for this seems to lie in the properties of shape (Rose *et al.* 1972, Meltzoff and Barton 1979). It is the *unlearned*, innate capacity to perceive and use shape as an organiser of experience upon which the identificatory and learning processes of the baby seem to be built.

From her clinical experience of autistic children Tustin had also arrived at the primary and innate significance of shape but she had difficulty in conceptualising the nature of the disruption which resulted in the autistic child's being unable to make use of his capacity to identify shape as an organiser of perceptual experience. Following Mahler, and Klein, it was difficult for her to depart from a two-person psychology in formulating a theoretical account of her observations. What she saw as a primitive disruption of the processes of perception and *awareness*, she conceptualised as a perverse *reaction* to awareness of bodily separateness from the object.

Tustin's dilemma was similar to that of Klein, when she struggled to account for the behaviour of her patient Dick (Klein 1930). Klein was clear that the boy presented a diagnostic and theoretical problem, because he 'failed to make emotional contact' and because of a 'lacking object relation'. In 1930, thirteen years before the publication of Kanner's paper and in the absence, therefore, of an alternative theory, she continued to try to accommodate her puzzling observations within the existing object relations scheme. Klein was tentative in her conclusions, but suggested that, 'The ego's excessive and premature defence against sadism checks the establishment of a relation to reality and the development of phantasy life.' She saw in Dick 'an inhibition in development and not a regression' and this is comparable with Tustin's massive 'shutting out' and 'not-knowing' defence.

The idea of a massive defensive withdrawal or a perverse manoeuvre, which effectively obliterates the meaningfulness of the animate object, raises a question of cause and effect. Is it the object that is shut out or is there an underlying more fundamental problem of failure to comprehend which results in *being* shut out from meaningfulness? Tustin comes near to the latter conclusion when she describes autism as a defence against unpredictability (Tustin 1991).

In a paper revising her views on psychogenic autism (Tustin 1991) she sums up her understanding of autism as 'a system of protective but alienating auto-sensual aberrations which have developed to deal with an infantile trauma of seeming to be wrenched away from a mothering person's body'. It is 'an early developmental deviation in the service of dealing with unmitigated terror'. Psychic development is arrested and the autistic child finds security in what then becomes an unregulated random world, by adhering concretely to autistic sensation objects. The mindlessness inherent in this experiential situation is well supported by the experimental evidence of recent cognitive research (Baron-Cohen *et al.* 1985, Frith 1991).

In the debate about autism and its aetiology, it is probably Wilfred Bion's Theory of Thinking which comes closest to taking account of the level of primitivity involved in autism. Whether the autistic state is considered in terms of a cognitive deficit (Rutter 1983), an inability to process stimuli meaningfully (Hermelin and O'Connor 1970), a failure of object constancy (Anthony 1958), a lack of empathy (Hobson 1986), or the absence of a theory of mind (Baron-Cohen *et al.* 1985), Bion's theory deals with a level of functioning subordinate to and therefore common to all. How far Tustin's conceptions of autism match the theoretical models of her analyst is the subject of much of this book.

Chapter 4

Unnatural children

'How unnatural!' is an exclamation of pained surprise which some of the striking instances of insanity in young children are apt to provoke.

Maudsley (1879)

THE DIFFERENTIATION OF DEMENTIA AND IDIOCY

The first classification to be established in childhood psychopathology was that which distinguished between mental illness and retardation when in 1838 Esquirol differentiated dementia from idiocy. Dementia was borrowed from the nosology of adult pathology and idiocy was a term which Esquirol reserved for those with a congenital defect in whom he saw no hope of recovery. He considered the prognosis for recovery from dementia to be greatly improved because of the possibility of repression of the symptoms (Esquirol 1838). This significant distinction was strongly disputed by Seguin, who made extravagant claims for recovery from retardation, but the views of the latter were led more by personal conviction than by science and his claims failed to be demonstrated (Seguin 1846).

Throughout the nineteenth century, both in this country and in America, opinions were divided on the aetiology of psychological disturbance in children. Increasingly, the neurological and psychological immaturity of the child came to be taken into account and began to replace the more global concept of insanity, associated with irreversible deterioration.

Attempts were increasingly made to distinguish between organic and psychological factors. Some saw the causes of childhood insanity in 'unstable' nervous systems, others took an environmental view, seeing trauma and early life-experience, such as prolonged deprivation or neglect, brutal parenting, or punitive religious teaching as implicated in the mental disorders of children. Some were convinced of the presence of organic damage and found support among others, who believed that true psychosis could not occur in children at all, since delusion, a primary symptom in dementia, required advanced cognitive capacities for its formation. Immanuel Kant, writing in 1798 about the classification of mental diseases, was uncompromising in his belief that all forms of derangement were inherited – 'There are no disturbed children'!

Prior to Kraepelin's reformulations in 1896, the understanding of adult psychosis was fragmentary and while one or two disease entities had been singled out, the condition was usually referred to in undiscriminating and depreciatory terms, as madness, lunacy or insanity. Childhood mental disorders, presenting a clinical picture which was even more difficult to comprehend, attracted still less attention. In 1883, a review of world literature on mental illness in childhood yielded just 55 papers (Clevinger 1883).

There were notable exceptions in Europe, where sporadic anecdotal reports had already begun to appear across the continent, describing the history and behaviour of certain 'mentally deranged' children. Some of these case studies reveal early indications of interest in psychogenic and emotional factors in childhood mental disorder and in this respect seem ahead of their time (Oesterreicher 1540, Mercurialis 1583, Brouzet 1674). However, it was not until the developments in the theory of adult dementia started to take shape that the further study and classification of childhood lunacy became possible. Kraepelin's work was highly influential and although he himself had little to say about children, his concepts were put to use and gave an impetus to the investigation of 'unnatural' children.

THE GROWING RECOGNITION OF CHILDHOOD PSYCHOSIS

It was Henry Maudsley, the pioneering British psychiatrist, who first attempted to introduce a nosological system of childhood psychosis into general psychiatry. He proposed a number of categories based on his observations of symptoms of disturbance which he correlated with the developmental level of the child and he saw developmental immaturity as a significant contributory factor in childhood mental illness. Maudsley came under considerable attack in 1867 when, in the first edition of his textbook *The Physiology and Pathology of Mind*, he included a chapter on 'insanity of early life'. Till that time, it was widely believed that psychosis could not exist in children because, it was thought, their neurological and psychological immaturity would ensure that any disturbances of development would be smoothed out in the natural course of maturation.

There was outrage at the very suggestion of the existence of childhood psychosis but Maudsley recognised in this hostile response the depth of fear and the aversion which could be aroused in adults by the spectacle of the bizarre and uncomprehending behaviour of psychotic children. He understood the sense of helplessness experienced in the face of the difficulties of understanding and treating such children. Gross aberration in the young, those in whom growth and development are taken for granted, is shocking and incomprehensible. The *sine qua non* of childhood mental life is challenged.

Kanner, whose own views attracted hostile criticism from some quarters, saw Maudsley's contribution as a landmark from which the reaches of childhood psychosis began to be explored and charted (Kanner 1954). Maudsley's place in the history of childhood psychopathology is rarely noted nowadays, but despite the inauspicious reception given to his first systematisation of 'early insanity', childhood psychosis, very soon afterwards, came to be widely accepted as a legitimate field of study.

Kraepelin's contribution to the classification of adult mental illness was to distinguish four separate syndromes which he named catatonia, hebephrenia, simple deterioration and paranoia. Some of these had already been identified, but in grouping all together under the comprehensive and unifying name, dementia praecox, Kraepelin introduced a nosology which survives to this day. He believed that psychosis was an organically based degenerative condition, involving the metabolic or central nervous system. His theoretical work did not extend to the consideration of childhood psychopathology but it did encourage interest in the study of the dementias in children. It was not until the twentieth century, however, that child psychiatry came into its own and the study of childhood psychosis, rather than being derived from adult psychopathology, began to contribute to its understanding.

Investigating mental disorders in institutionalised children, De Sanctis noted in 1906 that psychotic behaviour could occur in feeble-minded children as well as in those of good intellectual endowment. To differentiate the latter, he introduced the term dementia praecocissima as an indication of the very early age of onset of dementia praecox. He concluded, in contrast to Kraepelinian theory, that the mental decline associated with dementia was not necessarily degenerative but could also be regressive in origin and therefore reversible. This was an important diagnostic step, for it not only differentiated between organic and emotional aetiology in dementia but it introduced the concept of regression. In those cases where dementia was considered to be organic, the prospect of recovery was as bleak as that for idiocy. The idea of a pathological regression, on the other hand, held out the prospect of treatment. This brought the maturational processes to the fore in the search to comprehend mental disorder and opened the way to twentieth-century developmental psychology and psychologically based research.

AUTISM AND CHILDHOOD SCHIZOPHRENIA

Bleuler's revision of dementia praecox in 1911 not only changed the terminology but broke away from Kraepelin's view of psychosis as an organic, deteriorating condition. He introduced the term schizophrenia to replace dementia praecox but, like Kraepelin, he discerned a cluster of syndromes and so spoke, not of a unitary schizophrenia, but of 'the group of schizophrenias'. Influenced by Freud, Bleuler diverged significantly from Kraepelin in attributing importance and meaningfulness to the psychological features of the psychotic symptoms. His understanding of the psychotic manifestations as having both defensive and adaptive functions added a new dimension of clinical insight. In addition he formulated a diagnostic specification which became known as the 'four As' for the diagnosis of schizophrenia. These were Affective disturbance, Autistic withdrawal, Ambivalence and Associative (thought) disorder.

Bleuler brought to the incomprehensible world of insanity the idea that there might be structure and meaning in psychotic symptoms, but it is striking that he, too, disregarded entirely the pathology of children. His ideas stimulated great interest in all psychosis and at first the 'four As' were applied, unmodified, to childhood mental disorder. It was not until 1933 that Potter produced diagnostic criteria which took account of the differences in onset and clinical course which were specific to children. Potter's criteria for childhood schizophrenia were:

1 generalised retraction of interest from the environment;
2 disturbances of thought, manifested in blocking, symbolisation, condensation, perseveration, and incoherence;
3 disorders in language function sometimes with mutism;
4 diminution, rigidity and distortion of affect;
5 excessive or inhibited motility, leading to incessant activity or reaching the point of immobility;
6 bizarre mannerisms with a tendency to perseveration or stereotypy.

Despite these differences to which Potter drew attention, the term schizophrenia began to pass into general use in referring to the mental disorders of children. The premature use of this diagnostic label may itself have prejudiced progress in the study of childhood mental illness, contributing to the ensuing controversies and confusions about aetiology and terminology. The 'resistances to the existence of *schizophrenia-like* derangement in little children' (Mahler 1958 – my italics) have not entirely disappeared and this may have been the result of rushing into conclusions based on similarities and paying too little attention to the differences between the phenomena of adult and childhood psychopathology.

The first major advance out of the diagnostic morass of derangement and unnatural behaviour in children was Kanner's delineation in 1943 of the syndrome Early Infantile Autism. For the first time, it was possible to consider that some meaningfulness and order lay concealed in the seemingly lunatic world of psychotic children, and psychotic children themselves were being distinguished from others with learning difficulties of different origins.

Kanner's work was shortly followed by that of Margaret Mahler who in 1949 began to differentiate syndromes of childhood psychosis on the basis of failure to achieve certain specific intra-psychic structures in infancy. She introduced the concept of 'symbiotic psychosis', distinguishing between those children who formed some degree of relationship with other human beings, however crude or confused, and the autistic children, whom Kanner identified by their 'extreme aloneness' and their indifference to other people.

Mahler and her group spent most of the 1950s on her extensive research investigation into the factors which influence pathological development in infants. Studying large cohorts of healthy and disturbed children, Mahler concluded that the experience of symbiosis with the mother, or the mothering person, was the basic essential in healthy psychological development. She saw symbiotic unity with the mother as providing a psychological womb which facilitated the baby's psychological growth and its emergence into awareness of a mental world (Mahler *et al.* 1975).

The birth of the psyche is closely associated with the mother's physical care of the baby and its needs. Her physical ministrations are essential to the promotion of the sense of self and self-boundary; the 'self', as Bion puts it, not a mind in a body but a self with physical and mental attributes. Following in Freud's tradition (Freud 1923), Mahler saw healthy psychological birth as having as much importance to the future development and well-being of the child as its safe physical parturition. Since then, the importance of the mother's function as a post-partum psychological womb, which can contain her infant's emotional turmoil until personality strengths develop, has been increasingly recognised.

Mahler's classificatory work retains its usefulness today, not least in the mixed and confused area of learning disability. In this population, behavioural disorder and subsequent management problems are prominent. The most effective contribution to management technique comes from accurate psychodynamic assessment and clarification. Tustin's work has done much to bring a common touch to the understanding of 'unnatural' children, in a way which helps carers as well as psychotherapists to make greater sense of their task. In the next chapter, two cases will illustrate how an understanding of the logic-less world of psychosis can have a significant impact on the caretaker's perception of and response to disruptive behaviour. To be released from imputing motivation and intent where none exists is a relief to the carer and the therapist alike. Thinking is liberated and the nature of the problem being experienced can be given fresh appraisal.

Chapter 5

Encapsulation and entanglement

Footfalls echo in the memory
Down the passage which we did not take
Towards the door we never opened
Into the rose-garden.

T. S. Eliot, 'Burnt Norton' (1935)

Tustin's work, deeply influenced by her Kleinian training, is also built squarely on Mahlerian foundations. She became familiar with the work of American child psychoanalysts during her year at the James Jackson Putnam Center and had the the opportunity of meeting Mahler and her associates as well as Kanner. Well acquainted with the American debate on constitutionality or 'innateness' in childhood psychopathology (Rank 1949, Goldfarb 1956, Bender 1969), Tustin has always been careful to allow that some autism may be organic in origin. She delimits her interest specifically to psychogenic factors in autism but is in accord with Mahler's caution in linking infantile psychosis with a certain constitutional vulnerability. Tustin's forte, however, lies in bringing to Mahler's research findings a degree of clinical acuity and imagination which enlightens and enlivens the arcane world of childhood psychosis. From her Kleinian perspective, she has looked more deeply into the phenomena of autism and sketched her view of the unconscious dynamics. The result is a sensitive picture vibrating with echoes of inchoate experience which many of her readers have found recognisable in themselves.

In her first book, Tustin lists the differential features of autism and childhood schizophrenia, of the encapsulated and the entangled children as she termed them. Her experience in treating early psychosis led her to the view that both the psychotic child and the autistic were immured in a sensory world, unable to reach an experience of psychic reality.

Feeling states have not evolved and this then leaves them trapped in emotionless isolation, deprived of their humanity. It is a world in which the animate is not distinguished sufficiently from the inanimate and this interferes with the development of a sense of coherence and predictability. As a result, the achievement of meaningfulness in human relationships is seriously compromised.

Encapsulated children are usually in good physical health, with well formed, graceful bodies yet stiff and unresponsive to being held. They are alert, to the point of hyper-sensitivity, nimble and deft. High intelligence is often revealed in their behaviour and in their ready grasp of certain games or activities involving spatial relationships like jigsaw puzzles or computer games which do not require an understanding of personal relationship.

They have a history of early withdrawal, sometimes associated with screaming fits or tantrums. They may be mute or echolalic, after some initial language development. They are frequently fascinated by mechanical objects and become engrossed in spinning, ordering or arranging objects or toys, without regard to their function. Tustin sees these children as having opted out of life, arrested in their development, with a view of their mothers as 'closed down'. Because of their withdrawal behind a cold, hard, frozen exterior, both parents and clinicians often use shell metaphors to describe encapsulated children and Tustin characterised them as 'crustacean'.

Entangled children are much more likely to have had a history of poor health with respiratory, digestive or other physical difficulties. They are often clumsy, ill-co-ordinated and careless but, initially, relatively easy to rear because of their compliance. Their bodies mould easily in response to physical contact and being held. Eyes are often unfocussed and their thinking is confused with primitive fantasy. Intelligence is difficult to assess because of fluctuations in performance. There is some language development but speech is often slurred or indistinct. Confusion between self and other is considerable, both in terms of body boundary and in the degree of differentiation between self and external object.

Tustin regarded these children as regressed rather than arrested and found that their confusion of identity made them much more difficult to treat. She saw their relationship with the mother as too open and lacking in boundary, allowing the child to become excessively invasive. She used the model of an amoeba to indicate the amorphous fusion and confusion of these children's relationships and their disorderly development.

Like Mahler, Tustin views autism as a sensation-dominated state of being, resulting from an impoverishment in emotional nurturing (whether environmentally or constitutionally determined). Mahler stressed the importance of bodily sensations as the 'crystallisation point of the feeling self, around which our sense of identity will become established' (Mahler 1968). A sensori-emotional conjunction is required for sensation states to make way for feeling states and the role of the mothering person in this is crucial. This is where Mahler saw the necessity of a symbiotic experience from which the psychological birth takes place, enabling the infant to enter into the mental world of the psyche. There may even be a critical time for this but, without the emotional link which makes possible a personal empathic and essentially human relationship with another mind, intellectual growth and development are fundamentally and seriously impaired.

Tustin's two themes, encapsulation and entanglement, describe, respectively, the states of autistic withdrawal and psychotic confusion. She saw autism (and psychosis) as an extreme reaction to trauma; the trauma which Mahler envisaged in the failure of symbiosis. Ejected 'untimely' from the psychological post-natal 'womb', autistic withdrawal from human reality appears to be the final protective manoeuvre for survival; the child's human potential encased in the hard, uncaring crustacean exterior.

There is an intrinsic problem in trying to convey the quality of pre-verbal experience which prompts such drastic measures.

Fright comes close, a concept distinct from fear, which carries the notion of the existence of an object to be feared. Fright which includes shock and unexpectedness is consistent with what is commonly understood by trauma. Primitive, pre-verbal experience, beyond the containment of words, has been described by Bion as 'nameless dread' (Bion 1967) and is probably the best description available for this primitive, atavistic fear. Bion's phrase conveys both the degree of terror and isolation involved and the total absence of any hope of salvation. Signally, Bion's description also contains the indication of the direction in which hope might lie, i.e. in the civilising potential of the name, were it to become available. Identification is the corollary of naming and is the prerequisite of differentiation and discrimination.

What is dreaded is the experience of uncontainment, of unboundedness in uncharted space. Winnicott has referred to fears of 'falling endlessly' and links this with the primitive infantile fear of falling which can at times be reactivated in falling asleep (Winnicott 1958). Autism is, for Tustin, a defence against the premature and unbearable awareness of the separateness and otherness of the object. She regards Kanner's syndrome, Mahler's symbiotic psychosis and what others have termed childhood schizophrenia as having in common one fundamentally autistic characteristic: their dislocation from reality, particularly the reality of other sentient beings. In this sense, the lives of such children could be termed 'unnatural' in that they have broken away from the natural biological order and the source of their humanity. A dislocation so primitive, without intention or motivation, seems to defy nature.

It is important to appreciate the difference between loss of an object and loss of the possibility of contact with an object. The object has to have been found in order to experience its loss; that is, the pre-conception of an object has to have found its realisation (Bion 1962b). Tustin (and Mahler) makes clear that the void experienced in psychosis is of a different order from loss of the object. A disruption which occurs between the pre-conception and its realisation, between the innate expectation and the fulfilment, means that the loss is not something which is clear and meaningful but is the more deeply lost by being covered with confusion. Tustin finds in Winnicotts' understanding of this catastrophic breakdown of contact something similar to her own clinical experience with autistic children:

> For example, the loss might be of certain aspects of the mouth which disappear from the infant's point of view along with the mother and the breast when there is separation at a date earlier than that at which the infant had reached a stage of emotional development which could provide him the equipment for dealing with loss. The same loss of the mother a few months later would be a loss of object without this added element of loss of part of the subject.
>
> (Winnicott 1958)

Winnicott called this *ultima Thule* of depressive experience, psychotic depression. It is the 'black hole' or 'pit' frequently referred to by depressed adult patients from which the possibility of a return feels to be in great peril. (The 'black hole' phenomenon is discussed in greater depth in Chapter 6.) In this world of blackness, hope has not been lost, it has been extinguished. The experience is often likened to falling into a bottomless pit – 'I had to claw my way up again, inch by inch,' said one patient.

The return thus achieved did not mean that my patient was restored to normality, for the 'fall' was contingent on the precariousness of her pre-existing object relationships and much strengthening work remained to be done. The frail quality of such relationships is frequently concealed by pseudo-relating or 'false-self' development (Winnicott

1960) and often goes unrecognised until breakdown. In symbiotic psychosis, however, the false-self formation fails to develop as a defence because early splintering and fragmentation of the ego precludes splitting of the self into two.

This brings us to the confusional states which Mahler associated with a second type of reaction to the trauma of separatedness. In the syndrome which Kanner referred to as a 'pure culture sample of inborn autistic disturbance of affective contact' (Kanner 1943), there has been a paralysis of dependency feelings in the child, but Mahler finally came to the conclusion that symbiotic psychosis was also a defence against dependency and a similar terror of human attachment. In this case, the capacity for human attachment is not petrified inside the child as in the encapsulated child but, instead, its dim recognition is incorporated and held on to by the skin of the teeth with a tenacity that allows no differentiation between self and object. The blurring of self and object in this way is now the defence against the threat of separatedness and lies this time in fusion and confusion with the object and a very different quality of denial of separateness.

The relationship bridge is lost again but in a quite different way. Fusion with the object is clung to with ferocity in an effort to deny separateness and the intensity of this has to be recognised and appreciated. Many workers have mistaken fusion with the object for relatedness and have paid a heavy price. In such cases, whether children or adults, instantaneous switches of feeling can occur between all-embracing affection and ruthless aggression. Over-closeness can be of a very different order from closeness. The difference is not simply a matter of degree any more than the difference between neurosis and psychosis. There is a qualitative difference of perception which has as much clinical significance and is as important to appreciate as the difference between neurosis and psychosis of which it is an indicator. The implications for treatment and technique are critical. An excellent example of the psychodynamic significance of the differences has been described by Padel:

> A regressed patient in hospital could not be fed by nurses because he kept pushing away whatever was offered to him. He kept his face and mouth protected from the advances of the spoon by holding his arms out in a defensive circle. He would let nothing pass over this barricade, moving it up or down to fend off all attempts to feed him. Finally, Dr Padel thought of passing the spoon *underneath* the defensive barrier and the patient began to eat without trouble.
>
> (Padel 1978)

The difference for the patient lay in his experience, not of being fed from an outside source, but (as if) from inside, without the need to recognise the existence of an object on whom he was dependent. In avoiding the recognition of his dependency on an external source of nutrition, he was maintaining a delusion of being back inside the maternal object in an intra-uterine phantasy.

Tustin found entangled children much the more difficult to treat. The 'hard nut' of encapsulation may be very difficult to crack, but in entanglement the further defence of fusion and confusion with the object means that the therapeutic task is complicated by perversity. The masquerading 'relationship' with the object conceals and softens the same hard core, but it is a manic and evacuative way of relating. This fills the therapeutic space and threatens to smother the therapist's thinking in the service not of communication but of densifying the defence. It is a mockery of relating, incorporating the object and blotting out the separate identity of the 'other'.

In the case of the encapsulated child, the potential for relationship is impacted and may possibly remain intact. With entangled children, a capacity for relating has suffered a serious perversion. This conceals in softness and fluidity a murderous hatred of the reality of the object and of all human relationship by creating a semblance of object contact. The confused nature of this quality of object relationship lies in the susceptibility to reactions of instant hostility which spring up whenever awareness of the dreaded experience of separateness, so feared and hated, is threatened. Figure 1, a drawing by a five-year-old patient, illustrates the defensive enclave thus created. Fusion and confusion are maintained with an intensity which produces a barrier which, though soft and fuzzy, is as formidable a task to penetrate as the autistic 'shell', if not more so.

Two brief case illustrations will demonstrate the differences between encapsulated and entangled children and the different conditions encountered by those who attempt to help them. Both of these children were attending special schools for children with learning difficulties. Both children had severe learning problems but both gave their teachers a strong impression of their good basic intelligence. In the one case, the difficulty for the teacher was in establishing and maintaining the most fragile of contacts. The child, a girl, hardly used language. In the second case, of a boy with an adequate vocabulary, but whose speech was indistinct, impotence and frustration for both teacher and child predominated.

Figure 1 Drawing by a five-year-old illustrating the nature of the entangled child's relationships

J, AGED NINE

> Go, go, go, said the bird: human kind
> Cannot bear very much reality.

T.S. Eliot, 'Burnt Norton' (1935)

The classroom was empty but for the teacher and one other child besides J whom I had been called to assess. A boy, also manifesting autistic features and prone to outbursts of severe destructiveness, lay on a mat in the sunshine by a window, with J lying close by. They had their backs to one another and J's face was turned away from the direction of my approach.

I began by speaking to the teacher who was feeling relieved that the children were, at least, calm and undisturbed and who did not relish the possibility of stirring up new trouble.

I called 'hello' to J but there was no response. She might have been deaf although I knew that that had already been suspected and had been investigated.

There was a sand tray in the middle of the room and I decided to seat myself by that to see what, if anything, might ensue. I began by running sand through my fingers, and within a few seconds there was a stirring of J's legs as she, barely perceptibly, moved position. I said nothing and continued to focus on the sand. I took a toy funnel and wheel which was lying in the sand tray and began to pour sand into it, making the wheel go round. In a moment, J raised her head slightly but did not look in my direction and lay down again. I felt I was being watched in the most surreptitious manner. It was hard to believe that she could see me at all from where she lay, but her movements coincided with my actions.

I went on pouring the sand and J's interest began to show, growing very very slowly over the next fifteen minutes. First, she sat up and watched, then she came into the middle of the floor and finally she came and sat down at the sand tray. At first, she seemed to be just there, not taking the slightest notice of me. It was as if she had arrived there quite fortuitously.

Next, she laid her face on the edge of the sand tray and dangled a hand absentmindedly in the sand. Then she sat up and began to toy with the sand, letting it run through her fingers.

All this time, I had gone on playing with the sand-wheel by myself but I now took a second wheel and set it up close by, leaving it standing in the middle of the sand tray. In a few minutes, J began to pour some sand into its funnel and gave a squeal of delight when the wheel started to go round. We both then continued to pour sand into our respective funnels for a time, until I decided to pour some sand into her funnel. She stopped to observe this but did not look at me; then she returned to pouring her own sand in, as if nothing had intervened. I then ventured to pour some sand on to the back of her hand as she played, but with that she jumped up from the chair and flew off like a startled robin, back to her place on the floor mat, curling up again with her back to me.

My attempt to introduce myself into her world was too much and, at that point, perhaps too crude as well and I was firmly shut out again. In this child, an appetite for life and human relationship survives but is all too easily abandoned when she is frightened off. Her approach is made not simply with caution but as if she could join me only on condition that no link between us is to be recognised. She could approach curiously provided I remained indistinguishable from the inanimate wheel and her explorations could be managed and controlled by her eyes. As soon as I

broke into the detachment of that observatory world, drawing attention
to my live existence, I had instantly to be excluded. Like Padel's patient,
J had to maintain a delusion of absolute self-sufficiency.

Words, had I spoken to her instead, might have preserved her isolation a little longer, for she had a striking capacity to ignore the functions
of her ears, as was apparent when I arrived. As it was, she could no
longer shut me out of her awareness, except by taking action. From her
infancy, it had been difficult to believe that the child was not deaf and a
considerable amount of time had been given to the investigation of
deafness in this child.

This vignette of her way of relating to the world demonstrates how
important it is for her to be able to keep watch. As soon as there is an
experience which breaks through her looking and draws attention to
other sensations, she flees. It seems likely, in my experience, that the
maintenance of psychotic and autistic isolation is closely associated
with over-reliance on the eyes and the visual mode of perception and I
shall return to this later in the book.

THE FRUSTRATIONS OF ENTANGLEMENT – THE CASE OF B

B was twelve years old when I first met him and he had been living in a
residential unit for several years. He sometimes went home to stay at
week-ends but from about the age of four the family had found him
unmanageable. It was also clear to social workers, called to the case, that
there was little parenting capacity available in the parents and that parenting
for that couple would have been difficult, in the best of circumstances. The
problems presented by B swamped them and they could not manage him at
all. He seemed to be totally beyond their influence.

He had developed language but his speech was indistinct, his words
ill-formed and slurred and his sentences fragmented. He was similarly
unco-ordinated in his body and clumsy in his movements. He was
commonly regarded as lazy.

Both teachers and care staff were convinced of the boy's intelligence,
not least because of the wiliness he showed in getting what he wanted.
Classical Autism, as described by Kanner, seemed to be contradicted by
the fact that there were things he wanted and sought to get for himself,
particularly food, and he understood that he could also use people to
achieve his ends. He was also capable of a minimal degree of concentration and he had learned to read and count a little.

In special schools for the learning-disabled, children like B stand out
as showing some potential and this is welcomed by their teachers, who

are otherwise faced largely with the task of educating all those children previously deemed 'ineducable' prior to the Education Act 1983. In such stony educational ground, entangled children attract teaching interest and, understandably, excite enthusiasm. Unfortunately, initial confidence soon turns to frustration and disappointment and the entangled child can sap the morale of teachers bent on teaching someone who seems to be capable of learning, and appears only to be lazy.

I arrived on a routine visit to one such teacher and was greeted with relief. 'Thank goodness you've come,' she said. 'He's been terrible today. He was climbing up, trying to jump out the windows. I don't know what to do with him. He's dangerous.'

The teacher had been giving a reading lesson and she and B were alone in the room. I saw that she had been seated on one side of a table with B on the other, hemmed into a corner. It was clear that he had no escape, except through the windows!

The teacher, pleased that B could read a little, was determined that he should improve his skills and had been trying to get him to complete the present task which she regarded as well within his capacity. She saw his refusal as laziness and tried to insist that he concentrate and get on with the work. When he kept getting up from his chair and wandering round the room, she had moved the table to the corner in order to keep him there, in an attempt to show him that, with a little concentration, he would succeed. However, the more she insisted on controlling him, the more desperate this child became, and the more resistant he became, the more determined she was that she would show him that he could succeed if only he tried.

She was totally unaware of the escalation of terror her tactic was bringing about. What she saw as sustained persuasion in the service of teaching him to concentrate, he, as a child who could bear very little emotional contact, experienced as traumatic persecution and he was driven to desperation. By the time I had arrived, the teacher was driven to sitting on the table in order to restrain the boy from climbing up to the window sill.

It was not easy in this case to introduce an alternative perspective, for the teacher was convinced that she was engaged in a trial of strength and it was some time before she could believe that the child might be in a state of terror.

Ultimately, after some careful consideration of the teacher's perspective and the introduction of a new interpretation of the boy's behaviour, a considerable improvement of approach was achieved. When this child's (and others') limitations were better appreciated, the result made for a more benign classroom atmosphere and revived the teachers' morale. Moderating expectations, not the same as encouraging laziness, as was feared, did not reduce the level of achievement and did much to enhance classroom communication and co-operation.

Balance is difficult to gauge and maintain with such children. Disciplined order and routine are essential to counteract confusion and to foster a sense of security and predictability. The child's co-operation cannot be assumed on the basis of periods of friendly co-operation, for this can switch to hostile rage in an instant, whenever an experience of frustration has to be tolerated. This is not ingratitude, nor is it vindictiveness, and to make such a mistake escalates tension in the direction of panic.

What is required is a stable, holding response which can weather the child's outbursts and frustrations without flinching but also without adding to the persecution. Such a response requires a very high degree of maturity and sophistication in the caretaker or teacher, whose own emotional balance and morale can be severely tested by entangled and entangling children.

Chapter 6

Mental cataclysm and black holes

Psychosis is not primary process without a repressive ego; psychosis represents the presence of bizarrely transformed primary and *secondary process. Psychosis is not merely primitive; it is bizarre.*

Grotstein (1989)

Well before astrophysicists first reported their discovery of black holes in the cosmos, Frances Tustin was learning from her three-year-old patient, John, about the 'black holes' of his experience. Tustin presented this clinical material in her first book and opened up a whole new area of theory and technique for psychoanalytic investigation (Tustin 1972). She went on to develop these ideas in subsequent books (Tustin 1981, 1986) and her study of 'black hole' phenomenology became her most important contribution to psychoanalysis. She was closely followed by other psychoanalysts who began to note references to similar experiences in the material of patients suffering from primitive mental disturbance (S. Klein 1980, Kinston and Cohen 1986, Grotstein 1986). Psychotic patients, it seemed, had long since been familiar with 'black holes'.

Grotstein, like Tustin an analysand of Bion, has advanced our theoretical understanding of the psychotic's world in a detailed psychoanalytic examination of the phenomena of 'black hole' experience (Grotstein 1989). He acknowledges the seminal contribution of Tustin's work with autistic children, which has complemented his own subsequent findings in his analysis of adult patients with primitive mental disorders. I am much indebted to his exposition of the parallels between the scientific use of the concept 'black hole' in astronomy and physics and the use of the term as a psychological model, with its archetypal connotations.

Grotstein has developed his own and Tustin's ideas, carrying forward their thinking in a way which presents us with a modification of Freudian and Kleinian theory to encompass the psychology of powerlessness and its psychopathology. Psychoanalysis, based traditionally on a different paradigm, involving power and the conflict between the mental apparatus and the demands of the instinctual drives, has always associated psychopathology with the psychical destructiveness of envy and guilt and the defences against it.

Both Tustin and Grotstein see the trauma of nothingness and meaninglessness as the nadir of human experience. Annihilation of the sense of existence, loss of the very matrix of identity, with an ineluctable descent into a state of nothingness and meaninglessness, is seen as the most dreaded human experience, not psychosis, which, on the contrary, appears to proffer the last defence against it. This fundamental 'nil' experience, described as a black hole, the abyss, the void, is one which is associated with organismic anxiety and is the epitome of trauma. Existential fright reaches beyond psychotic anxiety, bringing a new and more primitive depth of fear where 'fate' more than 'guilt' is paramount. The greater threat is not from the irruption of instinctual drives into the ego but from the terror of impending disintegration or dissolution of the self and objects and the advent of chaos and meaninglessness.

THE EXISTENTIAL THREAT

Many other psychoanalysts and thinkers have noted and studied this level of ontological insecurity, but none has been able to enlighten so obscure an area of the human mind as well as Tustin has done through her sensitive studies of the experiences of autistic children. Her images of the world as experienced by the autistic child, shutting out all 'not-me' experience and becoming immured in a sensation-dominated prison, are graphic and evocative. Her writing communicates with the directness of poetry and carries deep conviction. Convictions, however, need to be supported by evidence and by theory and this becomes a matter of exceptional difficulty when pre-verbal experience is the subject of study. Concepts are deeply complex and intrinsically difficult to communicate and to understand.

Sartre's *Being and Nothingness* was published in 1943; the first philosophical work to discourse upon personal psychical experience and the sense of existence. In 1946 Spitz wrote of the severe level of withdrawal from life which he had observed in institutionalised children, to which he gave the name 'anaclitic depression'. Bibring (1953) called this 'primal' depression. Winnicott (1960) talked of an infantile psychotic depression in which there was a threat of 'failure to go-on-being'. For Laing, writing in 1960, implosion, fear of engulfment and petrification presented the most extreme ontological threat to the human mind. Mahler (1961) saw infantile depression as the experience which 'ushered in' the psychotic break with reality, while Bion (1962b, 1963) described a psychological catastrophe.

According to Bion, this infantile catastrophe institutes a profound split in the personality, a split very different from that engendered to defend against depression. This splitting constitutes discontinuities of experience and is perhaps more precisely termed slicing (Riesenberg 1990). It is most readily recognisable in the capacity to hold incompatible ideas simultaneously.

Because violence of emotion is not differentiated from destructiveness, the links between feeling and thinking are severed and 'a split between psychical and material satisfaction develops' (Bion 1962b). There is a negation of emotional being which is contingent on the destructive attacks on the mental links which allow meaningfulness to come into being. Similarly, Balint's (1968) seismographic metaphor of a 'basic fault' refers to a profound fracture in the individual's capacity to experience the world.

However described or represented, there is a common line of agreement about the significance of a primitive early disruption to the inchoate psyche and the developing sense of self. When fear of aggression (whether from a subjective or an objective source) is strong enough to inhibit the infant's instinct to obtain sustenance, organismic distress brings about a chaotic state of turbulence. This disruption obtains at a biological as well as a psychological level. It is the precursor of psychosis which may or may not be capable of psychotic transformation; the developing psyche is under severe threat and the emerging self feels doomed.

The psychological transformation of this state, insofar as that is possible, is psychosis. If the disruption is pre-mentational or remains unmentalised and is not psychically transformed, an infantile autistic state ensues, in which elements of the primitive self survive in either an encapsulated or an entangled form, but essentially in a deadened state. In this way, the catastrophic split between thinking and feeling fulfils the objective of destroying awareness of all feelings, so that both breast and infant appear to be inanimate. This means that the self is no longer available for its primary identificatory and discriminatory function. Without 'the orienting beacon' (Mahler 1961) of the primary, live, object, 'the background presence of primary identification' (Grotstein 1980), that is, without the emotional relationship within which the primitive projective–introjective processes might begin to forge identification and meaning, a cataclysmic 'black hole' depression is experienced in which life becomes chaos, and is experienced as random. The innate predisposition to make the meaningful connections which contribute to the creation of a sense of continuity of existence is itself disrupted.

PSYCHOSIS AS A DEFENCE

The situation now requires a different dynamic system for its understanding. This is where Grotstein seeks to supplement psychodynamic theory with chaos and self-regulation theory (Grotstein 1989). The emotional turbulence which characterises all mental disorders and is specific to primitive disturbances is thus to be understood partly through psychodynamic theory and symbolic understanding and partly through the application of the laws of chaos theory.

Self-regulation is, he proposes, a dynamic system which accounts for stabilisation of the self at the bio-psychological and psycho-biological level. When distress is extreme but its nature or meaning cannot be recognised, the turbulence is modulated by auto-sensory and motor attempts at self-soothing. Although some of these activities might resemble the common maternal modes of comforting an infant, like rocking, the absence of such a concept in the autistic individual means that he is also likely to 'soothe' himself with injurious activities. Autistic rituals, stereotypies, self-rocking, all testify to the existence of self-regulation at this level when destabilisation of the fundamental sense of self is threatened. It is the last defence against a black hole of chaos and meaninglessness. Ritual and stereotypy serve in the attempt to plug a hole when the psyche is frozen with fright, on the edge of an abyss, and unavailable for the transformation of the trauma into the bizarre world of psychosis. Without the defence of psychosis psycho-biological homeostasis has to be achieved in the autonomic, constitutional, sensory-motor sphere.

In ordinary everyday life it is a part of the mother's function to impart to her infant an experience of the modulation and regulation of primitive panic and fear and this is included in Bion's concept of containment. He noted the paramount importance of the mother's capacity to contain and transform her infant's primitive fear of dying (Bion 1962b) into a bearable feeling. Winnicott's 'holding environment' focusses on the non-mentational function of the mother to bring regulation through physical comforting and soothing. Bowlby (1969, 1973, 1980) recognised that the establishment of meaningfulness was a significant factor in attachment and bonding. The autistic child's rocking, banging or tapping is not meaningful and is not mediated by an object. It is an attempt to self-regulate, through rhythm, the dread of falling endlessly, of running out, of dissolving or of disappearing. The autistic individual thus becomes locked into a chaotic world without meaning, which he experiences as random and to which he can respond only in desperate and mindless ways.

Mathematical theorists have now found that chaos is not random, but is subject to certain regulatory processes within its own force field. This has led Grotstein to postulate that psychosis is a disorder of self-regulation as well as one of symbolic dysfunction. He sees the traumatic state itself as one which 'approximates the experience of randomness and approaches cataclysmic meaninglessness' (Grotstein 1989). Chaos represents the slide towards entropy. Such a degree of disorganisation and loss of cohesion breaks through the domain of the psyche, and the disturbance is removed out of mentation into the somato-psychic, sensory-motor sphere, where attempts are made to regain a vestige of control. It is Grotstein's hypothesis, following Tustin and Bion, that psycho-biological stabilisation (sensory homeostasis) is a pre-requisite of the personal and emotional interactionality which leads to mental growth. From a basis of sensory stability and security comes the capacity to transcend the sensory-motor organisation which permits meaning to be generated and valued and psychic content to be born.

As in the astrophysical use of the term, which was coined in 1969 by the American scientist John Wheeler (quoted in Hawking 1988), psychological 'black holes' are to be distinguished from static voids. Grotstein speaks of 'the awesome force of powerlessness' which is expressed in an implosive centripetal pull into the void and Tustin also makes it clear that the 'black hole' is not an empty void but a space into which one has fallen or been dropped. The phantasy is of something having disappeared or been lost for ever. If the 'floor' of one's being feels as if about to collapse, that is without a feeling of sensory security and safety, there is a primitive fear of falling, falling into a void or a black hole.

This experience is referred to variously by patients as the abyss, a bottomless pit, dissolution or collapse. The term 'black hole' conveys a catastrophic discontinuity of the self, loss of the sense of being alive; a black, psychotic depression which consumes or engulfs the personality with a sense of losing the very floor of existence. But it is not only that. It does not simply represent catastrophe and psychotic disorganisation. It is not empty space but negative space; a world of perversions and reversals. It is the negative matrix of 'transformations in hallucinosis' (Bion 1962b) where the altered distorting laws of madness operate and where Bion's 'bizarre objects', 'nameless dread' and 'the ghosts of abandoned meaning' reside.

Freud's understanding of these negative processes as 'psychotic restitution' is well described in his account of the Schreber case (Freud 1911). When psychotic restitution fails, autism is the ultimate apocalyptic experience. Beyond the conflicts between meaning and negative meaning which find resolution in the distortions of psychosis lies the ultimate withdrawal from live experiences and the total psychic depletion which was recognised by Freud in his term 'decathexis'.

This final point of 'black hole' discontinuity of the psyche bears a striking resemblance to the mathematical calculation of a singularity within the cosmic black hole. 'At this singularity, the laws of science and our ability to predict the future would break down' (Hawking 1988). At this point of human bio-psychological collapse, the psychological matrix provided by the primitive introjective–projective processes breaks down, and with it the capacity to conceive internal mental space. In this event, the infant is consigned to a sensation-dominated world and relies on concrete, adhesive forms of relating to an object (Bick 1968, Meltzer *et al.* 1975).

Evidence for this state of affairs is now growing in the field of empirical research where it has been demonstrated that autistic individuals, uniquely, do not conceive of mental states. Autistic children seem to be incapable of, or severely impaired in their capacity to make use of, 'pretend-play' (Ricks and Wing 1975). They do not employ second-order representations but remain limited concretely to first-order representations of the world around them (Leslie 1987, Frith 1985). Baron-Cohen (Baron-Cohen *et al.* 1985) has demonstrated that autistic children do not have a capacity for empathy or imagination and this confirms the common observation that such children treat objects and people alike. They do not have a concept of mind and so do not conceive of mental or emotional states in others.

THE TUSTIN VIEW

Tustin's approach to understanding the blackness and deadness of autism seems far removed from the theories and abstractions of mathematics and astrophysics. Her conclusions are based on her observations of her own attempts to communicate with children who seemed to be positioned beyond comprehension and beyond concern for their isolation and entrapment. In her work with these children, she began to find that the object relations theory in which she had been trained was inadequate to help her when the problem seemed to be one of being rendered non-existent by the child, in a world of aberrance and perversion. Klein reported a similar experience with her patient Dick who 'ran round me just as if I were a piece of furniture' and she, too, was puzzled by the theoretical inconsistencies. Ten years before the discovery of autism, she could only conclude that the child suffered from 'an inhibition in development and not a regression' and this she ascribed to 'a complete and apparently constitutional incapacity of the ego to tolerate anxiety' (Klein 1930).

The psychopathology of deficit has to be distinguished from the psychopathology of defence and this is where Tustin had to introduce new techniques different from those in which she was trained as a child psychotherapist. Interpretations based on defensive conflicts and resistances did not address the very different problems she encountered. There was little to be gained, for example, in making interpretations concerning the content and meaning of the session, when the child seemed to inhabit a world without meaning and where the therapist's mental presence in the eyes of the child seems problematic. When words are being totally ignored, the primary task in such circumstances is to discover a way of marking the presence of the therapist so as not to be completely obliterated by the child. There is a pre-requisite need to engage the child and, if necessary, to 'reclaim' his attention (Alvarez 1980) in order to establish the meaningfulness of the session.

Tustin's experience of working with autistic children began with a veritable 'baptism of fire' when she joined the James Jackson Putnam Children's Center in Boston in 1954. There, she undertook to live with and care for autistic children in their own homes as part of the centre's respite care scheme, to give relief to parents. This experience left her with no illusions about the treatability of such wayward and bizarre children, yet she remained fascinated and challenged by the problem of re-establishing meaningful contact with them.

The years of clinical experience with autistic children which followed that first encounter culminated in a breakthrough of her understanding when she was treating the little boy, John, whom she refers to in all of her books. It was an experience which brought enlightenment, as she came to see the important distinction between loss of the object and the phantasied loss of the self. Her clinical experience with this little boy confirmed and gave meaning to Winnicott's thesis about early feeding disturbance in which he suggests that the loss of the nipple during the early nursing experience of fusion and confusion with mother can be experienced as a loss of a part of the mouth. It was this insight which provided a platform for her further thinking about 'black holes'.

PSYCHOLOGICAL BIRTH

Tustin uses a birth metaphor to portray her understanding of autism and sees the autistic child as having had to endure prematurely the on-slaughts of psychical reality, before an adequately holding mental structure has been developed. 'Ripped untimely' from the symbiotic psychological membrane, the autistic child has been exposed to emotional life 'in the raw', untransformed by a containing object to modulate and to give meaning to experiences. Instead of giving psycho-logical birth to a conception of mental space, in which relationships with live people are contained, there is a violent eruption into endless space, perceived as a black hole. One severely ill, obsessional patient said she felt she was literally surrounded by chasms which she was always in danger of falling into and this could be experienced in the session as she sat terrified to move out of the chair. The same patient had grown up feeling uncertain of herself, and either out of place or disapproved of. No doubt, herself, a difficult enough child to rear, her memory is of the failures of the object to provide security. She refers regularly to child-hood experiences of a constant fear of having things taken away from her by her mother, who used this as a means of control and punishment.

The birth of the psyche is closely associated with the mother's physical care of the baby and its needs. Her ministrations promote an important sense of self-boundedness. The 'self', as Bion puts it, is not a mind in a body, but a self with physical and mental attributes. 'The ego is first and foremost a body ego' said Freud, giving prime significance to bodily sensations (Freud 1923). Ogden has coined the term autistic-contiguous position to indicate the sensory basis of this most primitive of psychological organisations generating the sense of being (Ogden 1989).

Lacking even the sensual containment of enfolding, of rhythmic beat, of sensual hardness and softness, of periodicity that provide a sense of 'going-on-being' (Winnicott 1956), the infant is left alone to weather, as it were, a hurricane, a blizzard or a volcanic eruption. Against such odds, the massive withdrawal from the psychic to the sensory world which follows leaves a sense of total abandonment, as if left in the middle of a desert, or a post-nuclear wasteland, two images commonly found in the dreams of the borderline psychotic.

The crux of autism, says Tustin, is the tantrum. Paroxysms of rage, a white heat which melts down the personal empathic bridge upon which personality growth and development depend. Timing is intrinsic and critical. Tustin sees autism as a response to a very early trauma in which the infant is exposed prematurely to the reality of bodily separateness, before he has the mental equipment to comprehend it.

When the mother–infant couple cannot function in a way that makes bearable the awareness of separateness, then the resultant 'holes' in the 'emergent self' (Stern 1985) produce 'an agony of consciousness' (Tustin 1986) which is unbearable. Symbiotic nurturing is exploded away, demolished almost as soon as it begins to be a possibility. Unable to make use of symbiosis, the child is left stranded in a world of untransformed sensory objects. It is a world of inanition, originating in the need to be rid of an unbearable awareness of life and relationship with live objects. In this sensation-dominated state, emotional and cognitive development perish, while the autistic manoeuvres attached to sensation perseverate and rigidify. Pathological autism aims to eliminate the unknown and the unpredictable, by limiting relationships to the concrete and to what lies within the visual field.

In her analysis of the clinical material from her sessions with John, Tustin describes vividly how she came to understand his phantasies of devastating loss. Through John's use of a red button as a symbol of the nipple, she reconstructs what she understood as his omnipotent illusion of bodily fusion with the object in a teat–tongue cluster of oral sensations. The nipple, rather than the breast, is central to her thinking. It is the 'red button' nipple which becomes the symbol of the crucial symbiotic love object. If there is a traumatic impingement of reality *before* this sensory cluster becomes sufficiently differentiated into a nipple–tongue, mouth–breast conjunction, the potential for empathy and containment is destroyed, with catastrophic sequelae.

When the pre-conception of a nurturing object cannot be realised, there is no maternal matrix to provide a structure for the growth of identification. The feelings which bestow meaning on sensory perceptions cannot be generated. It is as if the neurological 'feeling self' (Miller 1978) had perished at birth and with it the capacity to identify with a caring object. Instead of a 'hatching' (Mahler 1961) from the symbiotic illusion of at-one-ness with the maternal object, the autistic child is prematurely exposed in an eruption from the safe shelter of the psychological womb into a frightening unbounded world of 'not-me'. The feeling self, petrified, is projected a very great distance.

The autistic individual's deadness is the result of this loss of the maternal function which means not only the loss of the containment of the object, but also loss of the 'transformational object' (Bollas 1979). Absence of the conditions for the transformation of life-events into the psychic entities of thoughts, feelings and dreams, means the loss of the processes fundamental to thinking to which Bion gave the name alpha function. Without alpha function, the unprocessed experience (beta elements) (Bion 1962b) remains neither mental nor wholly somatic but constitutes a tormenting gap or a hole in the potential for understanding and meaning.

Tustin has found many striking images with which to convey her understanding of autism. She affirms the psychological catastrophe to which Bion drew attention, but adds her own amplification, that psychological catastrophe is the result of a premature or mismanaged 'psychological birth' and that this trauma produces the cognitive inhibition and dysfunctioning which characterises the autistic and psychotic conditions. In the autistic child's bizarre behaviour, she catches a glimpse of the half-life beyond the catastrophe where the ever-present threat of 'black hole' depression looms.

Autism is an extreme condition, but Tustin has also opened up and articulated a level of experience which is recognisable and intelligible to psychotics, to neurotics and to some so-called normals. She has added graphically to the theory of catastrophe and she has drawn attention to the need for important shifts of therapeutic emphasis (technical and theoretical) which are made essential for the treatment of psychosis. She has even added her view that an autistic enclave exists in all patients which needs to be reached and brought to light, if real personal growth is to be achieved. These are significant insights, yet Tustin has not attempted to accommodate her thinking about autistic states into the body of existing psychoanalytic theory and it is not always clear in her books how they do fit in.

Chapter 7

The frontiers of consciousness

We need only say that there are two stems of human knowledge, namely, sensibility and understanding, which perhaps spring from a common but to us unknown root.

Immanuel Kant, *Critique of Pure Reason* (1787)

The new concepts introduced into child psychotherapy by Tustin found ready recognition and appreciation among a number of clinicians and by the 1980s she was beginning to develop a following, particularly in Europe. Her theoretical uncertainties were treated with caution among British analysts and child psychotherapists but there was at the time much more interest in psychoanalytic approaches to autism in countries abroad than in Britain, where autism and its treatment were dominated by Behaviourism and Learning Theory. Notwithstanding the clinical usefulness of many of her concepts, however, her ideas and constructions lay uneasily beside classical psychoanalytic theory. Was the deadness of the autistic child and the 'black hole' experience the *result* of 'excessive' projection or was there some even earlier failure which pre-empted the development of a primitive paranoid-schizoid organisation?

As more was being understood about autism as a disruption of the earliest psychological processes, more questions arose about how such phenomena and such theories fitted into the tradition of theoretical development from Freud through Klein to Bion and other post-Kleinians. In the last decade, a number of psychoanalysts have been looking more deeply into the nature of the primitive anxieties which comprise the paranoid-schizoid position, still widely regarded as the most primitive form of psychological organisation (Meltzer 1968, Rosenfeld 1987, Sohn 1985a, Steiner 1991, Joseph 1982). However, with the exception of Meltzer, most of these analysts have developed their thinking on the basis of their experience of treating adult psychotic and borderline psychotic patients and have not included people with autism. Tustin's writing, on the other hand, is based almost exclusively on work with children and she has concentrated on autistic and psychotic cases. The two approaches to the understanding of psychosis, advancing from opposite ends of the problem, are, so to speak, like the channel tunnel, destined to meet somewhere in the middle. The way through has been greatly advanced by the clarifying work of Grotstein (1985, 1987) and Ogden (1989).

Tustin (1972, 1986), Bick (1968), Meltzer (Meltzer *et al.* 1975) and Rosenfeld (1987), all influenced by Bion, applied his theory of container–contained to the understanding of psychotic and autistic levels of disturbance, recognising loss of identity and self-cohesiveness as the most profound anxiety. Some modification of Klein's theory of the paranoid-schizoid position seemed to be implied but was not elucidated and, with the exception of Meltzer's 'adhesive identification', there was no significant theoretical divergence or amendment. Tustin, herself, is not altogether clear about whether autistic children have been overtaken prematurely by primitive paranoid-schizoid mechanisms, their 'hole' created by excessive projection, or whether their psychotic 'hole' precludes the operation of even this level of functioning. She speaks both of explosive projections and of the absence of primal bonding.

Reiterating Tustin's emphasis on the significance of body-centred modes of experience, Ogden has proposed an autistic-contiguous position, to represent the human being's most primitive mode of experiencing a sense of 'self'. This stresses the fundamental importance of a world of sensory experience which is essentially pre-psychic, but is a vital precursor of psychic life and mentation. Disturbance at this level of sensory groundedness, which renders the very 'floor' of one's being unsafe, creates psychic havoc. It dissipates the emergence of a sense of bodily containment, the pre-requisite of psychic containment.

In Ogden's view, the paranoid-schizoid position can no longer be regarded as the most primitive level of personality organisation and he proposes a new term, autistic-contiguous position, to represent a more primitive level of experience belonging to the primary sensory modes of experiencing the object. Bion made an important addition to the Kleinian theory of the depressive and paranoid-schizoid positions, when he drew attention to the existence of a dynamic relationship between the two, rather than their being regarded as positions in a developmental sequence. With his autistic-contiguous position, Ogden now introduces a third pole into the dialectic of experience and he acknowledges how much he owes to the work of Tustin, Bick and Meltzer for this conceptualisation (Ogden 1989).

The identification and differentiation of this ultimate edge of awareness from the primitive paranoid-schizoid experience, and lying beyond that level of anxiety, has significant implications. It belongs in the area of experience where meaning is first generated and it involves the organisation of sensory impressions into the psychic qualities of feeling or thought. The anxieties characteristic of this level of experience and transformation of experience take the form of fears about losing sensory boundedness, sensory integrity or sensory continuity and the terrors are of leakage or running out, of dissolving, or of falling for ever. Such organismic anxiety is specific to this sensory level of organisation and it is anxiety of this magnitude which predominates in autism and is being defended against in psychosis.

CONTINUITIES

Ogden conceptualises the autistic-contiguous position as the most primitive form of psychological organisation, operative from birth. Even the use of the term 'psychological' is problematical since the organisation concerned is of the pre-symbolic ordering of the raw sensory data into meaningful content. Bion used the terms alpha function to denote this primary activity and beta elements for the elemental data. He referred to this as 'proto-mental' activity, to take account of its mental primitivity. In tracing psychic development to these primitive sensory origins, Bion's thinking, together with the work of his followers, now provides opportunities for generating a conceptual bridge between the biological and psychological spheres of development. Scientific attitudes which hitherto have rigidly regarded these two realms of discourse as mutually exclusive have impeded exploration of bio-psychological links and developmental continuities.

Ogden's clarification of the place of sensory modes of experience in human psychological development proffers an extension of psychoanalytic theory in which human experience is now seen in terms of the interplay of three modes of psychological organisation, bringing succeeding advances in integrative capacity, yet retaining the distinctive forms of anxiety which characterise each level of organisation. The different patterns of anxiety relate to the nature of the experience of disruption or disconnectedness occurring within each mode of experience. In the depressive position, the disturbance is to whole object relationships. The feelings experienced are at an inter-personal level, with fears of harming or of being harmed by the object. Paranoid-schizoid anxiety concerns the threat of disintegration of the self or of the object, with fears of explosiveness and fragmentation of the self and objects. In the autistic-contiguous position, the disruption is to the very sense of existence where the experience of sensory cohesiveness and bodily surface containment is threatened and the anxieties take the form of terrors of leaking, disappearing, dissolving, or falling for ever. Primitive object relationships are threatened by fears of engulfment and fusion with the object while whole and part object relationships are disturbed by confusion with the object.

The potential for all or any of these forms of anxiety to create emotional disturbance or mental illness continues throughout life, their containment or disruptiveness influenced also by life events and experiences. The location and identification of anxiety as the central objective of psychotherapeutic treatment was greatly facilitated by Klein's understanding of the schizoid splitting mechanisms and this led directly to improvements in analytic technique. What is now being proposed is a further level of understanding which identifies even deeper fears emanating from unspeakable existential terrors and which are communicated predominantly in autistic non-verbal and pre-verbal form.

It is now postulated that enclaves of autistic functioning and 'black hole' paralysis may be a contributory factor in therapeutic impasse, negative therapeutic reaction and the problem of endless sterile intellectual dialogue where treatment has focussed on paranoid fears and has failed to recognise and appreciate the significance of autistic 'black hole' dynamics.

Whilst not referring specifically to autistic phenomena, Rosenfeld seemed to envisage something very similar when he emphasised that the central anxiety in psychosis was of falling or falling to pieces and he related that to the experience of birth and the relinquishing of the safety of the womb. For this reason, he insisted that the capacity to pick up the patient's non-verbal projections was essential to the treatment of psychotic patients (Rosenfeld 1987). Another, earlier, reference to the need to attend to autistic-level anxieties in neurotic patients was quoted by Tustin in a paper in which she also suggests the existence of hidden autistic encapsulations which impede psychoanalytic work (Tustin 1986):

> The sooner the analyst realises the existence of this hidden part of the patient, the less the danger of the analysis becoming an endless and meaningless intellectual dialogue and the greater the possibilities of

a patient's achieving a relatively stable equilibrium. Although the analyst has to live through a great deal of anxiety with the patient, I feel that ultimately the results make it worthwhile.

(S. Klein 1980)

In my own clinical work I have found that much obsessional behaviour becomes more intelligible when viewed in the light of the autistic experience (Spensley 1992). An anxious and importunate woman, for example, who always came to her sessions with a lengthy agenda, seemed to be leaving no stone unturned as she deliberated on what was wrong in her life. She talked earnestly about what needed to be changed, how she felt she had been helped by me and again how I was not helping her. She regularly despaired that there would never be sufficient change in her fear of men for her to be able to get married and have children.

The session was always full of material which I would try to understand in terms of the underlying dynamics. Eventually, one factor began to emerge which seemed to have nothing to do with all of this material. Difficulties in ending the session began to increase to a disturbing level and she might take up to ten minutes to get out of her chair at the end of the session. I thought of her dissatisfactions with me and also of separation anxieties, both of which I took up with varying short-lived effects on her behaviour. It was not until I had recognised that the whole session and its verbal content was functioning as a barrier to contact with me, preventing not facilitating communication, that I was able to make a change of vertex (Bion 1962b) and bring into focus the terror of contact which had been totally obscured by her importunity. A vital but highly vulnerable self remained encapsulated and protected from me with the result that in that part of her experience she was not having a session at all. Instead, she gave a good performance of being a patient.

At first, my patient was ready to feel hurt and outraged that I could think of her as not participating in the session at all, despite all her apparent interest and eagerness for exploration. She did finally agree, however, that this did match her experience but added that if she were to have to take in what I said there would be no room and she had very real fears that she would literally burst. I shall have more to say about this obsessional patient later. For the moment I merely wish to illustrate how the most meaningful communication was non-verbal and that it was not until my recognition that a powerful underlying autistic shutting out of contact with me was perverting the function and meaning of the session that we were able to move forward in the work and she could begin to leave the session normally again. I had not until then noticed how much more significance was being placed on seeing me in the session, than on hearing what I had to say.

DEATH INSTINCT AND FEARS OF EXTINCTION

Ogden's theoretical contributions have greatly helped to bring Tustin's intuitive ideas of a primitive sensory world within the tradition of psychoanalytic theory, and in a similar way her notion of 'black hole' experience has found a place in Grotstein's extension of the theory of the death instinct. Both of these American authors acknowledge their indebtedness to Tustin's clinical intuitions but there is also a reciprocal benefit, in their clarification of how her new and original concepts might be accommodated within the existing theoretical structures.

Grotstein's work, as has already been described in Chapter 6, adds his perspective on primitive paranoid-schizoid fears by identifying a new dynamic of powerlessness and meaninglessness in the 'black hole' experience. He gives a definitive account of another distinctive level of mental organisation which he clearly differentiates from and views as more primitive than the paranoid-schizoid position and in this complements Ogden's work on this experiential frontier.

Affirming the death instinct, first formulated by Freud (1920) and endorsed in the Kleinian theory of primary sadism and destructiveness, Grotstein sees the death instinct as a 'signifier', in the Lacanian sense (Lacan 1973), of a deeper terror – death of the psyche, 'the fate worse than death' – in other words, as conveying an inherent preconception and apocalyptic pre-perception of such a 'black hole' fate. The death instinct concept is thus intensified, to include the warning of imminent death of the psyche and spelling the extinguishing of the human spirit, existential annihilation, loss of humanity (the 'signified'). The response that constitutes the final desperate defence against this catastrophe is psychosis. From this point of view, psychosis has a significant but neglected positive function in ensuring self and species survival.

Marrying the concepts from astronomy relating to galactic space with this extension of the death instinct concept, Grotstein sums up the position as follows: 'The death instinct, in other words, constitutes our reminder that we all cringe on the "event horizon" of "annihilation's waste" – with entropy (meaninglessness) and nothingness as our companions' (Grotstein 1989).

Tustin, Ogden and Grotstein are all concerned to move psychoanalytic enquiry to the very frontiers of human experience and to the edges of our human understanding. Tustin emphasises 'the heartbreak at the centre of all human existence', namely the awareness of bodily separateness which comes with the necessary psychological birth which must follow parturition, and Ogden has focussed on the earliest mode of generating experience. In Grotstein's view, the infant is born into a 'depressive position' of primary meaninglessness from which it is rescued by two agents. The first is the mother's capacity to provide containment, understanding and emotional nourishment and the second is the infant's own capacity to employ its paranoid-schizoid mechanisms to regulate and modulate initial non-organisation. To this end, the infant may avail itself of the inherent predispositions providing there is a satisfactory maternal environment and no pre-emptive interruption, from whatever source, to interfere at this embryonic level. Bion's preconceptions (Bion 1962a) or Jung's archetypes (Jung 1919) are innately available to impart primitive prey–predator meaning, thus countervailing the development of disorganisation and chaos.

Among those analysts who have applied Klein's concept of projective identification to the understanding of psychotic patients, Rosenfeld focussed on the confusional states induced by failure to differentiate self from object and love from hate (Rosenfeld 1950), of which we hear echoes in Tustin's term entanglement. Bion has extended Klein's concept of projective identification to differentiate an abnormal outcome of the paranoid-schizoid experience in a pathological form of projective identification (Bion 1962b). When this occurs, paranoid-schizoid splitting is replaced by minute fragmentation, and projection is used to evacuate rather than to communicate mental contents. Bion does not use the term 'black hole' in his thinking but he does envisage a catastrophe with the resulting non-containment analogous to an expanding universe or uncharted galactic space. Meltzer's concept of a 'dismantled' state in autism presents a similar picture in which the sense of experiential containment is lost and the sensory input is disconnected or dismantled (Meltzer *et al.* 1975). In American slang, the phrase 'spaced out' captures something of this sense of unboundedness.

My own view is that in such a state of evacuative non-containment, and in the absence, therefore, of the means for thinking, the eyes take the lead. No correlation of experience is possible and all objects, animate and inanimate, are 'known' and 'controlled' by watching. The development of the eye has played a major part in our evolutionary history, and in the animal kingdom seeing is believing. Reliance on this primitive mode of functioning in the world is, I think, what is resorted to in mental disorder and it is this 'tunnel vision' which forms the basis of concrete thinking. It is true of the autistic child, it is true of the paranoid patient and it is highly characteristic of obsessional behaviour, where it can be an agony to let things go out of sight (see above, pp. 59, 68, 125).

Several analysts, whilst not alluding to the phenomena of autism, have been interested in investigating the deeper levels of paranoid-schizoid anxiety and this has led to greater understanding of and respect for the complexities of the paranoid-schizoid position. In addition to its defensive function in keeping depressive anxiety and guilt at bay, there is now an appreciation of its protective value in maintaining a balance against overwhelming anxiety, helplessness and despair. The dynamics of a mental power struggle have been conceptualised as the organisation of parts of the self against itself in what is seen as a sado-masochistic attempt to maintain a precarious command (Meltzer 1968, Rosenfeld 1971, Sohn 1985a, Steiner 1987). Rosenfeld has likened this to a mafia-like organisation of the self and Joseph (1982) goes on to examine the self-destructive phenomena involved. She sees a relentless addictive pull towards what she terms a 'near death' state of being. Such patients, she posits, are enthralled by an unconscious fascination and excitement with the experience of being held in limbo and, as a result, become trapped in a form of 'mental brinkmanship', as they struggle to maintain psychic equilibrium (Spillius and Feldman 1989).

Questions remain about whether the destructiveness of pathological organisations of parts of the self is primary or defensive. In her review of developments in Kleinian theory, Spillius concludes that there is some consensus that they represent a compromise, 'simultaneously expressions of death instinct and systems of defence against it' (Spillius 1988). Joseph emphasises as crucial the addictive power of masochism, while Bion considers envy to be the primary destructive force. Klein, too, regarded constitutional envy as the most destructive and intractable influence on personality development. Meltzer, however, looks beyond the stranglehold of addiction and submission to a tyranny, to the inherent dread of loss of protection incurred by daring to rebel against the persecutor (Meltzer 1968). Where, he says, there is dread of loss of an addictive relation to a tyrant, the force behind the dread will be terror. In terror, fear for survival is activated but the attribute of terror that is crucial and noxious is its intrinsic paralysis and the dread is the dread of helplessness.

The new perspectives on paranoid anxiety presented by contemporary authors share common ground in their perception of a powerful struggle within the ego to maintain a balance between life affirmation and death instinct. Whether destructive impulses are to be seen as primary or defensive, the outcome of envy or masochism, it seems to me that the restrictions of this theoretical dilemma are relieved and to some extent advanced by the introduction of 'black hole' theory and the dynamics of powerlessness, loss of meaning and predictability. A longing for life too painful to bear may lie deeply hidden in envy and masochism, and interpretation of destructiveness may bury it more deeply. Meltzer considers the object of terror to be the phantasy of dead internal objects which cannot be escaped (Meltzer 1968). Escape from emotional consciousness in life, even at the risk of falling into the meaninglessness of a 'black hole', then seems to beckon as an alternative to the ordeal of discovering unbearable truth and feeling. The outcome is the same as in 'addiction to near death' but the dynamic is different. In all its perversity, does the 'liveness' in sadism defend against the 'living death' of autism?

Chapter 8

Of objects: concrete, sensory and transitional

Without sensibility, no object would be given to us, without under-standing, no object would be thought. Thoughts without content are empty, intuitions without concepts are blind.

Immanuel Kant, *Critique of Pure Reason* (1787)

HARDNESS AND SUBSTANTIALITY

Tustin's elucidation of autistic 'objects' and their pre-eminently sensory significance is her second major contribution to the understanding of primitive mental states. Autistic objects are not toys nor are they to be confused with Winnicott's 'transitional' objects (Winnicott 1958). When Kanner first described his group of autistic children, one of the features to which he drew attention was the manual dexterity of many of them and the excitement and gratification they seemed to derive from manipulating, spinning and whirling toys and objects: 'Donald and Charles began in the second year of life, to exercise this power by spinning everything that could be spun and jumping up and down in ecstasy when they watched the objects whirl about' (Kanner 1943).

The special attraction in such activities appears to lie in the rhythmic movement produced and some autistic children get equally excited by fluid properties and pouring. A marked feature of this obsessional interest in rhythm and movement is its hypnotic power. Children thus engaged are almost impossible to distract and if anyone tries to come between them and the engrossing object of their attention aggression and tantrum are likely to break out. The following clinical excerpt conveys the degree of absorption and the intensity of these preoccupations:

> From the beginning, Kate chose to immerse herself in two special forms of play. One involved water and paint, the other sand. These

activities had in common, a preoccupation with pouring, flow and dispersal and they were also distinctive in the similarity of the physical reaction which each evoked in Kate.

The paint was used by Kate to form puddles of colour on the basin ledge. These she would then encourage to run in little rivulets down the inside of the basin into the clear water below in which the streaks of colour would swirl and eddy until all their initial form and colour had dispersed in the water. At the point of total dispersal, when she would then pull out the plug, her physical involvement intensified and she would flap her hands wildly and loosely from the wrists as the water ran down the drain. In a similar way, she became engrossed in the flow of sand through a funnel, her eyes fixed in fascination as she poured the sand through the funnel over and over again and this was, once again, accompanied by the same desperate flapping hand movement.

(Spensley 1985a)

Autistic objects are not played with, nor are they endowed with imaginary qualities in the way normal children treat toys in their games. A toy car, for example, may be used predominantly in the upside-down position with interest focussed solely on spinning its wheels, or it could be carried around, held tightly in the hand, to give a hard edge sensation in the palm, and, in contrast to the choices of most children, such toys may be taken to bed in preference to the traditional teddy or cuddly animal. Concrete autistic objects used by children are invariably hard and this differentiates them importantly from transitional objects which are always soft.

Tustin makes descriptive use of the personal pronoun 'me' to include all the subjective flux of subject/object sensations experienced by the infant in its first weeks of life, before subject and object are clearly distinguished and differentiated. The autistic object does not, therefore, involve the child's conception of it as an object, nor of its having the properties of a 'thing'. The autistic object is used in an auto-sensuous way, as a means of ordering and delineating experience, in the course of which subject 'me' gradually emerges from all that is object and 'not me'.

Infants of a few weeks old behave similarly as they get to know the properties of objects: pushing, poking, rattling, beating, mouthing, examining in studied detail whatever comes to hand. In normal development, objects treated in this way facilitate learning; in pathological autism, the object that becomes an autistic object inhibits development. The objective ceases to be exploration of an external world; on the contrary, the aim becomes the absolute elimination of all that is unknown and unpredictable and the obsessive activity with the object is to ensure insulation from that world of 'not me'. In autism, these early developmentally important exploratory drives become stultified and rigidified into a compulsive sensory circle, which the child is driven to indulge in, repetitively and without meaning, in a way that blocks any further meaningful contact with the 'not me' world. In other words, the objects of the senses cease to be the desired and needed mother and the sensations themselves become the autochthonous 'objects' replacing and obliterating dependency on an external world.

The syndrome of pathological rumination is paradigmatic of the perpetual self-sufficiency and the self-enclosed circularity of pathological autism. In infantile rumination, the infant appropriates to himself the sensations of being fed and creates through regurgitation an illusion of containing the source of feeding, thus eliminating awareness of real dependency on the breast as the source of nourishment. Gaddini and Gaddini describe in graphic detail the essential difference between involuntary and spontaneous regurgitation common in early infancy and the purposeful bringing back of swallowed and partially digested food:

> Unlike regurgitation, where the food runs out of the infant's mouth without any effort, in rumination there are complex and purposeful preparatory movements particularly of the tongue and of the abdominal muscles. In some cases the hard palate is stimulated by fingers in the mouth. When the efforts become successful and the milk appears on the back of the pharynx, the child's face is pervaded by an ecstatic expression.
>
> (Gaddini and Gaddini 1959)

TRANSITIONAL OBJECTS

The transitional object is used to facilitate separation where good external objects are available but where internal confidence in the object remains problematical. The teddy or other soft cuddly toy is universally recognised as a comforter for young children but favourite blankets or pieces of fabric can also serve to bolster confidence. One of the best known of these is that belonging to Charles Schultz's popular toddler, Linus, who is always depicted trailing his 'security blanket' from which he is inseparable.

The transitional object is object-related (in the Kleinian sense) or object-directed. It is a substitute for the object, bridging the gap of separation that has to be tolerated to attain inter-dependence and maturity. The hard autistic object reassures at a much deeper level, that of suffocating or disintegrating anxiety in the face of loss of internal structuring and the sense of self. The hardness and edgedness of the autistic object is self-related and provides a sensation of substantiality, reassuring of the existence and continuity of the self, not the object. The hard autistic object helps, therefore, to defend against organismic panic and the 'black hole' of the psychotic terrors of running out, dissolving or disappearing.

BODILY CONTAINMENT

Skin sensations of hardness restore a feeling of boundary when the self feels threatened with the loss of sensory boundedness. My own view, which I would add here, is that at this frontier of experience, loss of identification with the body is threatened as a result of intense identification with the processes of elimination. Accordingly, losing one's mind is presaged by a fear of parting company with the body. The need to stay rooted in the body is paramount and the hardness of toy cars, marbles, stones, tin lids, etc., serves to offset the sensations of leakage and running out which are associated with psychotic depression. Compare George III's retort in response to tactful comments about his 'frame of mind': 'What do you know of my mind? Or its frame? Something is shaking the frame, shaking the mind out of its frame. I am not going out of my mind, my mind is going out of me' (Bennett 1992).

Physicality is part of one's human *and animal* identity and the significance of this was reaffirmed by Freud when he reminded that the formation of the ego ultimately derived from bodily sensations, particularly of the skin surface which yields perceptions that may be internal or external, that is, the experiences may be of feelings or of sensations. Freud saw the ego as a mental projection of the body surface and to some extent this bears comparison with Penfield's neurological projection, the 'cortical homunculus' (Penfield and Rasmussen 1950). 'The ego is first and foremost a bodily ego' (Freud 1923).

The schizoid individual often maintains a degree of aloofness from his body, commonly taking himself for granted in that physical respect. One patient, an artist, arrived for a session in a state of high indignation. He had sprained his ankle badly on an escalator the day before and had had to seek treatment. Recounting his experience, he protested with utter incredulity, 'I wondered what had happened? Looked down at my foot. The bloody thing wouldn't work any more! I couldn't walk.'

In the paranoid-schizoid mode of experience, the skin surface is, in phantasy, treated as a protector, like a suit of armour behind which to take refuge from a primitive and diffuse sense of danger. At the furthermost end of this spectrum, the body's needs may come to be totally ignored, a recognised concomitant of schizophrenia and regressed psychotic states. In this extreme, the patient becomes oblivious of the body's condition and deteriorates into a state of physical neglect.

Out-of-body experiences also feature in the reports of some borderline patients, and some people report clear recollections of the experience of being outside their bodies, usually feeling located somewhere above, looking down on themselves. More common are descriptions of ill-defined but no less frightening forms of depersonalisation or derealisation. An obsessional-compulsive patient who had been severely mentally ill for many years of her early adult life told me of an even more distressful extremity. She recalled a time when she felt she was in danger of losing completely parts of her body. She suffered severe mental illness throughout her adolescence and early adulthood and there was a time when she could not get out of bed because she would be overwhelmed by fears that she was losing parts of her body whenever she tried to leave the bed. The compulsion to be checking incessantly that her body was complete and in a safe enough condition to permit her to do so resulted in her being unable to leave the home for five years. During that time only alcohol and bottles of Benedrene, of which she consumed three bottles a day, could contain her panic and make her life bearable.

Many years later, markedly improved, but still dominated by checking, she was distressed in a session by my use of the metaphor of 'floating', an experience which she immediately recognised, saying, 'I'm detached. It's not really *my* body. I don't have any feelings. I'm most in touch with my legs, I think, because I do a lot of walking, but not my feet. I can't feel them.' She said she was still constantly afraid that she would 'float away, in a thousand pieces. I'd just be gone.'

My interpretation that she seemed to be checking her very existence was greeted with surprise and pleasure and she declared with astonishment that she had at that moment stopped checking for the first time in eight years. The checking resumed again in that session but that had been her first relief from it in all that time. It also marked the beginning of a gradual and continuing diminution in the virulence of her compulsive disorder.

Outside the realms of mental illness, phenomena of detachment from the body are sometimes experienced in life-threatening situations of illness or accident when severe pain is experienced and/or the body's survival is problematic. In certain religious cults, such experiences are regarded with special reverence and elevated, as a 'higher' form of consciousness.

The containing functions of the skin and its sensations in providing a primitive experience of boundedness were first put forward by Bick (1968). She suggested that at the earliest stage of personality and body-ego formation, the parts of the personality had no inherent binding force and that this derived from the experience of the skin as the container, parts of the personality being indistinguishable in the beginning from the parts of the body. Feeling shattered or overwhelmed and fears of literally falling-into-space or coming to a 'dead end' are not at first differentiated, in Bick's view. The experience of the skin surface as a primitive binding force carries, therefore, a primal containing function and she further postulated that any deterioration in the sense of cohesiveness of the skin would precipitate the development of a 'secondary skin' formation as a substitute. The muscular system is commonly employed to this end but Bick considered that the choice of the compensatory defence was intimately linked to the characteristics of the maternal care.

In addition to 'secondary skin' containment, Bick has also described how the loss of skin integrity may also be partially offset by adhesion to the surface of the object, thus creating a delusory sense of containment. Meltzer (Meltzer *et al.* 1975) added to Bick's concept of adhesive identification the notion of two-dimensionality to refer to the defensive use of adhesion to the object in the service of allaying fears of disintegration. Here, both Bick and Meltzer recognised clinical phenomena which challenged Klein's theory of the paranoid-schizoid position, a view they shared with Tustin, but did not carry so far.

The views of all three are complementary, and over-arched by Bion's Theory of Thinking and alpha and beta mental functioning. Bion has placed emotion at the centre of thinking and Tustin now gives prominence to sensibility and the necessity of a sufficiently safe and secure experience of being, to enable mentation to proceed. Ogden's use of the name 'autistic-contiguous' position indicates this more primitive level of psychological organisation and an important third mode of functioning that pre-dates the paranoid-schizoid position. It is in this sensory-dominated mode of experience that the boundedness of human experience can be appreciated and 'the beginnings of a place where one's experience occurs' (Ogden 1989) takes shape. As we have seen, anxiety at this level or in this mode is of unspeakable terrors of spilling out, leaking or dissolving into endless shapeless space.

AUTISTIC SHAPES

In her later work Tustin draws attention to a second type of autistic object. Contrasting with the concreteness and tangibility of the typical autistic objects, these 'objects' are subjective, abstract and intangible and she gave them the name 'autistic shapes' (Tustin 1984a). The autistic child's sensitivity to shapes is well known in their dexterity with jigsaw puzzles. It is the shapes of the pieces rather than the pictures which are used and it is striking in how many cases the child's expertise can be as easily demonstrated with the puzzles placed upside-down, without aid of the picture.

Tustin discovered from many of her very young patients that there were other 'shapes' which held a powerful fascination. These were not objectively recognisable geometric shapes but rather a 'felt' shape, personal and idiosyncratic to the child. Shapes might be discerned in any of the sensory modes but they are abstract and to be distinguished from specific sensory recognitions, like sounds, smells, tastes, etc. She sees significance in these 'shapes' as formations of sensation, and the harbingers of a primitive notion of boundedness. Tustin assumes an innate predisposition to form 'sensory shapes' and here she is in harmony with much of the modern infant research which demonstrates that infants are pre-designed to seek out and engage in learning opportunities.

Tustin places a new emphasis on the significance of sensory modes of learning and of the centrality of an awareness of a 'self' and she sees autism as a pathological deviation at this elemental level of experience. Stern stresses the importance of the infant's fundamental experience of the processes of organisation (Stern 1985). His understanding of the development of learning is that it is consolidated through awareness of the process of emerging organisation, in what he terms the 'emergent sense of self'. This understanding of the growth of learning is a departure from the work of Piaget and subsequent learning theorists which identified successive developmental stages and the associated changes in the sense of self which each bestowed (Piaget 1937a). Stern, like Tustin, regards the growth of the sense of self as fundamental to cognitive development and vital to the capacity to learn (Stern 1985).

The 'emergent sense of self' and Tustin's sensory 'shapes' both belong in the psycho-biological arena of predispositions or motivations towards the creation of mental organisation. Tustin is unclear what processes are involved but speculates on the primacy of tactility and kinaesthesis in infant experience and the two-dimensionality of these early sensations. She differentiates between an *impression* of a shape and the formal recognition of visible properties, the experience of which might be shared. Pattern might convey better than shape the quality she wants to capture:

> The objects and processes were at the service of the autistic child's entirely personal idiosyncratic purposes. Like the bodily substances, they were merely shape-producing agents. They scarcely existed in their own right for the child. Some young autistic children are so unaware of the actual existence of objects that they try to walk through them as if they did not exist. In the same way, they listen to other people's voices, not as a communication but as a self-envelopment by lulling shapes. Thus they are often thought to be deaf, before they are recognised to be autistic. The children are capable of forming elementary percepts and concepts from their shape-making propensities but these are idiosyncratic to them and they are not very interested in them; they are so captivated by 'shapes'.
>
> (Tustin 1984a)

An obsessional patient said with enthusiasm, 'I have always loved words; not for their meaning, it's the sound of them.' Another was enthralled by colours and textures and would buy very expensive clothes which she did not wear and often in sizes she could not wear. Such sensitivity to the abstracted 'global' qualities of the object can also be used positively and contributes to artistic creativity in highly gifted individuals. John Gage quotes in his study of Turner, an observer's account of the artist's complete engrossment in such qualities:

> At the end of his life, too, Turner was discovered on one occasion among the Thames-side wharves beyond the Palace of Westminster and probably near his Chelsea cottage, 'squatting on his heels at the river's edge and looking down intently into the water'. Half an hour later, the same observer saw him still there 'and apparently, the object of his interest was the pattern made by the ripples at the edge of the tide'.
>
> (Gage 1987)

Tustin's own 'feel' for the predicament of autism is acutely sensitive but her intuitive approach leaves her, too, with a problem of communication and the verification of her views awaits greater scientific rigour. The common ground she shares with Stern and modern infant research lies largely unrecognised and Tustin's own paper in 1991 suggests that she herself does not fully appreciate the concordance. The discovery of the infant's capacity to co-ordinate perceptual information from different modalities has been a significant advance (Meltzoff and Barton 1979, Rose *et al.* 1972). Replicable experiments demonstrate that infants in the first weeks of life are 'predesigned to be able to perform a cross-modal transfer of information that permits them to recognise a correspondence across touch and vision . . . . No learning is needed initially, and subsequent learning about relations across modalities can be built upon this innate base' (Stern 1985).

Stern proposes the term 'amodal perception' for the demonstrated innate capacity of the infant to translate information from one modality to another. No experimental evidence is yet available to establish how this is accomplished and it therefore remains an open question whether Tustin's intuited 'felt shapes' will eventually be found to have a relevance to the way in which sensory information is represented and transmitted. Stern sums up the current research findings in words which echo those of Tustin when he draws attention to 'global' as distinct from sensorily specific qualities of experience. 'These abstract representations that the infant experiences are not sights and sounds and touches and nameable objects but rather *shapes,* intensities and temporal patterns – the more "global" qualities of experience' (Stern 1985 – my italics).

A sensory proto-mental system of awareness is what Tustin envisages and she postulates that it is the disruption of this inchoate process of mentation which results in the autistic's becoming imprisoned in a sensory-dominated delusional state, where his experience remains 'unmentalised' (Mitrani 1987) and therefore continually threatened with dispersion and dissipation. The level of consciousness is restricted and in her view tactile sensations take precedence in providing a sense of safety. The distinction between conscious and unconscious remains blurred. In Bion's language, a screen of beta elements is in operation, its elements unsuited to communication, and relief is found in actions and sensations which are self-stimulated and self-controlled.

Chapter 9

The keeper of the keys

The work of the therapist is to extricate himself from the mechanical constructions of the psychotic child.

Tustin (1981)

In this chapter I shall look at some of the treatment recommendations and the implications for therapeutic technique which derive from the understandings of autism and psychosis which have been described by Tustin. I shall bring these considerations together with material from one of her cases, so as to present, as it were, a picture of the psychotherapist at work. A certain amount of clinical material concerning the case of Peter has already been published in her book *Autistic States in Children* (Tustin 1981). I draw on this as well as on other published sources and supplement the whole with observations based on my clinical conversations with Frances Tustin.

IMPLICATIONS FOR TECHNIQUE

In the course of her clinical work with autistic and psychotic children, Tustin has evolved certain principles of therapeutic practice and technique. These emphasise the priority she accords to the regulation of the child's behaviour over interpretation of the symbolic meaning of the content of the session. The need for firmly defined boundaries of space and time is, for Tustin, the primary technical requirement. Where there is confusion of identity with blurring of psychological boundaries and/or inadequate differentiation between people and objects, it is imperative first to establish enough order and regulation of the therapeutic contact for the therapist to differentiate her presence and not allow herself to be treated like furniture. This means a more confrontative attitude and much greater firmness with children than has been the traditional practice.

The sense of self is rooted in bodily awareness and Tustin believes that this is encouraged by common-sense restraints. She makes it clear that she would not allow the child to misuse his own or the therapist's body. She would encourage orderly conduct, such as hanging up outdoor clothing on arrival or clearing away toys at the end of sessions. She expects beginnings and endings of sessions to be marked in formal ways with greetings and good-byes, in order to keep the boundaries of space and time in focus, and she discourages the bringing of the child's own toys to the session, for the same reason. These principles depart from the permissiveness and laissez-faire approach to the treatment of children advocated in the beginning by Bick, but they are now widely accepted and practised by child psychotherapists.

In these practical ways, Tustin feels she can encourage the child's awareness of the therapist in time and space and thus awareness of a world of other people. Similarly, since the primary objective in the psychotherapy of psychotic children is to bring the therapist's presence to life in the mind of the child, the therapy will initially focus on the behaviour which betrays the child's failure to differentiate between animate and inanimate. In the treatment of psychotic children, unlike neurotics, the therapist has to be much more active, striving to be perceived as a live object, and not allowing herself to be walked over, talked over and treated like furniture.

This means a marked change of therapeutic approach and technique, with the physical and behavioural communications of the child taking precedence over the verbal content of the session. That actions speak louder than words is nowhere more apparent than in the communications of the psychotic. As well as Bion, Rosenfeld has warned us of the necessity to attend to the non-verbal communication of psychotics – 'the capacity to pick up the patient's non-verbal projections is essential in the treatment of psychosis' (Rosenfeld 1987). The fundamental difference between autistic and psychotic children and those who are less disturbed, the difference which has such significance for technique, lies in the absence of conflict. In autism and psychosis, identity, and therefore intra-personal confusion, is the central problem and not conflict. The psychotic process creates a condition in which the personality is radically split and left *minus* that emotional life which would give rise to personal and inter-personal conflicts.

The absence of boundary which this confers in psychosis allays emotional conflict and resistance and the absence of conflict and discrimination also removes the need to differentiate between conscious and unconscious. Conflict is thus replaced by actions and enactments of that which cannot be mentally experienced. Enactments are not symbolic for the psychotic individual, although they do carry a degree of communication and function as symbols for the observer.

Where there is little differentiation between conscious and unconscious, interpretation can be, at best, confusing, at worst, positively harmful. For example, the interpretation of phantasy to a confused psychotic child may interfere with rather than add further clarification. Interpretations in such circumstances can be understood not as a clarification of reality but as a confirmation of the phantasy. A five-year-old psychotic boy whom I saw many years ago, when I was relatively inexperienced, talked throughout the session about heroic deeds and superior abilities. He spoke a lot about the wonderful garden he had which was far better than his dad's or his grandmother's gardens and he described how he could grow anything he wanted in it. When I commented on how he seemed to feel that he had magical powers and felt much stronger and bigger than the grown-ups, he was not brought down to earth but, on the contrary, agreed with fervent enthusiasm. The fires of his omnipotence were fuelled by my remarks and he added that he was even more exceptional than I had suggested; he had great big orange trees and grapes in his garden and he could fly up over them higher than Superman could go!

There was a certain seductive charm about this little boy, but he was so captivated by his phantasies that he had to be treated in a residential school. At that point, acting out of his phantasies had not reached a level of endangering life but this can be a real risk with paranoid patients. To interpret psychotic phantasies of persecution as if they were neurotic can be very dangerous indeed. If the patient does not sufficiently recognise the separateness and reality of the therapist, interpretation does not introduce reality and bind the phantasy, but, on the contrary, compounds the sense of persecution because the therapist is felt to belong in the psychotic world, knowing about and confirming the fears. Acting out in response to mounting fear in such a case can mean that to survive, something or someone must be destroyed.

This is a hazard which is largely circumvented in the treatment of the autistic and obsessional patient, because of the inherent concreteness of these conditions. However, Tustin's insistence on the primary importance of establishing firm and mutually accepted boundaries is no less stringent in these cases. In quite different ways, truth and reality are under attack in both autism and obsessionality but Tustin's priority in all cases is to uncover the psychotic 'black hole' terrors which, she believes, inevitably underlie the hostility and distortions of psychosis.

In the case of Peter, whose treatment I shall now try to follow, Tustin began with a child who gave little indication of being interested in anything she had to say. He hardly spoke in the early sessions and she was faced with the problem of engaging his attention' and, literally, of making her presence felt.

PETER AND HIS BUNCH OF KEYS

Peter was aged two years six months when his parents began to seek advice about his strangeness. He was first taken for investigation in New York when his parents had begun to suspect that he might be deaf. The results of all physical examinations proved negative but he was also seen at that time by Anni Bergman, a colleague of Margaret Mahler and co-author of *The Psychological Birth of the Human Infant* (1975). It was by coincidence that Tustin learned of Bergman's acquaintance with the case and in a personal communication with Bergman was told that he had been mute and extremely withdrawn at that time. He had shown the behavioural features – averted gaze, stereotyped hand movements and tip-toe walking – frequently associated with autism (Tustin 1981a: 221). On this report rests the diagnosis of autism. There was some further support from the impressions of a Manchester psychiatrist, who also considered the boy to be autistic and who was treating him contemporaneously with Tustin, in accordance with his own method of educational therapy which he called Functional Learning.

Peter was referred to Tustin by his parents and not through the more usual route of psychiatric referral. They were active in pursuing every possible source of help for their son. A well-to-do couple, he was their first-born and they were keen to support every treatment they could find that might help Peter. His parents were not even deflected from their objectives by the fact that the family lived in Wales, while Tustin lived and practised in the Home Counties. Arrangements for Peter's treatment had to be unusual, with the family undertaking to travel south every week-end, staying overnight in London so that Peter could have two sessions per week, one on Saturday and one on Sunday.

By the time Peter arrived to be treated by Tustin he was six years old, and the child she saw then was a rather hunched, screwed up, tense little boy who seemed weighed down by the bulk and weight of the large bunch of keys which he always carried with him. Tustin describes him as 'speaking in a very restricted way' and says that he 'could hold a pencil, but did not draw or write spontaneously with it' (ibid.: 221). He was an uncommunicative child but not so disturbed as not to be able to attend normal school and he also seemed to be responding to Dr Walden's Functional Learning.

Peter's parents were pleased with the progress he was making in his cognitive, educational therapy but thought that he still displayed a lack of emotional responsiveness. With hindsight, they thought that there had been an oddness and a remoteness in his behaviour from very early life. There were no exceptional events or traumatic experiences in his history but Tustin has recorded that his mother had been depressed when Peter was a baby and his father had to make frequent trips abroad on business.

Of particular interest in this account of his early developmental behaviour was the mother's observation that the baby had been a 'poor sucker' (ibid.: 223). This was of particular interest to Tustin who had just been alerted to the significance of early oral experiences in her treatment of John. In her presentation of this case material, she was already formulating a theory of the nipple–tongue interaction in suckling, as a paradigm of interpersonal development. However, as I have confirmed in my discussions with Tustin, she was aware of the gap that remained to be bridged between an intellectual and theoretical understanding of the pathology and the communication of that under-standing to the child. Her experience with John, she considers to have been fundamental to her thinking about autism and childhood pathology and it was this work which provided her with a ground plan for her treatment approach to Peter.

In the absence of personal communication with this child, she felt her point of contact lay in the bunch of keys and she talked to him about the importance and significance of the keys as a means of protecting himself (ibid.: 226). She saw the keys as the autistic object which was used by him to confer a sense of safety and strength.

EARLY SESSIONS

At the beginning of his therapy, Peter, like many autistic (and psychotic) children, totally ignored the therapist and Tustin describes feeling as if she did not exist in Peter's eyes. His averted gaze and his concentration on his keys, examining them and counting them, was capable of extinguishing her as a live object in the room and this drew immediate attention to her primary and most difficult task which was to find ways of making her presence felt. In Peter's case, Tustin did this in two ways. First by establishing a clear ritual of beginnings and endings to the sessions so that he could not avoid that boundary and, secondly, by creating for him a story based on his keys as the most prominent feature of the session.

Her method is to attempt to draw the child's interest in this way, by endowing autistic objects with emotional meaning. In this way, they may come to be invested with meaning for the child, so that his addiction to these objects as autistic plugs holding in the fear of leakage or dissolution is loosened. The transition to a more viable sense of security of self is achieved, she believes, by the dramatisation of her reconstructions of the child's early sensations and feelings. Her stories about the child's early experience, as she understands it, are told in a way that tries to bring to life the primitive atavistic terrors of bodily separateness and of being exposed to annihilating attacks. It is against such terrors that the autistic object is clung to, as a kind of talisman. For Peter, it was his bunch of keys which fulfilled this protective function and she would talk to him about his dire need to hold on to their hardness and substantiality as a means of protecting him from feeling soft, light, ethereal and vulnerable to dissipation or dissolution.

Little evidence is made available in her account of sessions to indicate how this kind of approach is received by the child, and indeed Tustin admits that it is a relief to her that changes seem to occur without her knowing why – 'It is a great comfort to me that much goes on in the therapeutic situation of which I am unaware' (ibid.: 141). Be that as it may, we read that this was how she proceeded with Peter and that she was rewarded one day, three months into treatment, when he moved on from handling and fingering the keys to using them like a template to draw around. It was a significant shift for Peter to start to use the keys as representable on paper by their outline. No longer were they being used exclusively in his idiosyncratic way as autistic objects to protect himself and to keep him feeling safe, or as autistic shapes to impress into his skin to help bestow sensations of comfort and strength. Now, there was a new possibility of looking together at representations of the keys and their more usual function, a function which was shared and not idiosyncratic to Peter.

At first, Peter took up the new activity with equally obsessive interest, repeatedly tracing the shapes of the keys on paper, as he had once counted and handled them. This went on for many sessions until about a month later, when a new drawing was introduced and this proved to be another moment of change. Peter drew the playroom chest of drawers in which the children's toys were kept and he drew the keyholes belonging to each drawer with a key placed alongside each keyhole. This enabled Tustin to make more direct links between her own constructions of his infantile experiences and his present thoughts and imaginings about keys and their uses. Now that the keys were being presented in their ordinary realistic function, they could be seen as providing a link between child and therapist and between child and other patient children, the users of the other locked drawers. Tustin notes the beginnings of a real relationship with Peter at this point, with her feeling much more of a presence in the room for him (ibid.: 227). I would add here that his interest in the chest of drawers and their keys also connected him with a conception of inside and outside and marked the beginning of an appreciation of Tustin as having life and a mind with mental contents about which he could now become curious.

AUTISTIC TAGS AND STOPPERS

Original notes of a session which took place soon after this breakthrough will now be quoted to illustrate the qualitative shift in Tustin's relationship with Peter. She begins to feel more of a real person for him and he, at least, seems to consider that he has someone to talk to. He hears her, but whether or not he is listening at this point is another matter. The session which follows came four months into therapy, at a time when Father, who was often away on business, was about to return:

Peter entered the room carrying a banana, encircled by his hand, proudly and triumphantly saying, 'Look what I've got!' As I looked at it, it seemed to be much more than a mere banana. It seemed to be growing out of his hand and to be part of his body. It was the way he held it and the triumphant gleam in his eyes which gave me this impression. Well, he peeled the banana and he ate it voraciously with great greedy gulps. He hardly chewed it, but let it slip down his throat, rolling it around his tongue as if it were part of his tongue. It was gone in three bites and gulps. As soon as it was gone, he looked tired and old. He looked at me pitifully and said, 'I've got a sore place.' As he said this, he touched his mouth and then said, 'on my arm'. He offered his arm for me to look at and there was, indeed, a small sore place. He said, 'Susan did it to me. She scratched my thing away from me.' He then went on to say, 'He [meaning "she"] is younger than me and she doesn't know any better.' It seemed as though he were repeating what his mother had said to him. He continued, 'He scratched me.' It was a small round sore place which looked to me like a bite. The whole speech was somewhat confused. I said I thought that while Daddy was away he and his mother had become very close together like it was when he was a little baby. Daddy coming back tomorrow stirred up the time when he had felt that the lovely sensation thing in his mouth, which connected him to the Mummy, had been snatched away from him by Daddy and later by Susan, his sister. He felt that losing it left a sore place. He said, 'What is a dinosaur?' I said that he felt that if he knew a lot of long words, like dinosaur, they would plaster over the sore place. He said, 'Daddy gave Mummy the keys so that she could lock up the factory so that no one could take anything.' I said that it made him feel very unsafe when he found that Mummy wasn't joined to his body. He was afraid that his mother was no longer locked up and that his things were not safe. He gave a strange reply to this saying, 'When the stopper came out of the bottle, I fell and fell and there was no bottom.' I said, 'Yes. It was very frightening when you found the nipple thing wasn't in your mouth like the key to lock it up.'

Peter went to the mirror and looked at his mouth and gazed at the gaps where his milk teeth had been. I said, 'Now that your first teeth are coming out, it reminds you of the time when you felt you had lost the nipple stopper from your mouth and you felt there was a gap, an empty space.' He said, 'I'll teach them to grow.' I said, 'There is a part of you that knows that you can't teach them to grow. That it is not under your control, to make them grow. You have to wait for them to grow.' He said in a forlorn way, 'I am the manager.' I said, 'It is hard for you to have to learn that things happen to you which you don't arrange yourself. You so much want to feel that you are in control of everything so that nasty things don't happen, like finding that you and Mummy are not joined together and that you have to share her with Susan, your sister, and with Daddy. In the same way, you have to share me with Arnold and with the other children. All that hurts and makes you feel sore.'

He was still at the mirror and he extended his tongue. As he looked at his mouth, he said, 'Boiler.' He had talked about boilers in other sessions. I hadn't found the significance of this to him. Suddenly, at this point in the session, I had a flash of intuition and I said, 'Oh, I know. Do you think that "boyler" is a boy with an extra bit to his body? Is that it?' He nodded, very pleased that I had at last understood.

I went on, 'When you were a baby you felt that the feeding thing on Mummy's breast or on the bottle was an extra bit to your tongue. Like you felt the banana was an extra bit just now.' He came and stood beside me, because I think he felt I was really understanding him now. When he felt like that, he had what he later called 'a conversation'. He stood beside me talking to me in a conversational way. He said, 'I used to go and see Uncle Tom.' Then, 'What is a partition?' I asked him what he thought it was. He said, 'Something that divides one room from another.' He then asked, 'Do you know what an intersection is?' I asked him to tell me what he thought it was, to which he replied, 'Where the road divides.' I said I thought he was feeling that he had to accept the fact that he was no longer part of Mummy's body, part of my body, but that we were divided from each other and that made him feel very sad.

However, at the end of the session, the realisation of our separateness was too much for him. I was sitting on the sofa with my arms folded, one on top of the other. Peter looked at my posture very carefully and then tried to copy exactly the way my arms were folded and my posture. I said that I thought that when the session came to an end, it was very hard to bear the thought that we were divided from each other and went our separate ways. He felt that if he looked like I did and copied exactly what I did then we were identical with each other and we were not separate from each other. He nodded sadly. When I said it was time to go, Peter went to the door with heavy steps. Later, Mother told me that Peter had seemed very tired following his time with me. In the light of this session, I believe she meant depressed.

(Quoted in Hedges 1994)

This session portrays Peter in more animated contact with Tustin, no longer excluding her, but still showing little evidence of emotional communication. She understands his comments about partitions and intersections to be about separatedness and interprets accordingly. She assumes depressive concern at this point but the recognition of this seems to be more in her mind than in his. What evidence there is, here, of Peter's state of mind, suggests an obsessional rather than a depressive concern. He is interested in how the therapist thinks and in investigating her mind but he reveals nothing of what he himself thinks or feels. His exclusive attention to external experience is consistent both with his initial diagnosis of autism and with an obsessional defence which would now indicate a distinct advance on the Bergman report of his demeanour at age two years. The keys are now firmly associated with their external function, but while other objects now become a source of interest and curiosity for Peter, their meaning and existence are located in the external world.

Tustin's expressed objective in treating autistic children is to encourage the child to re-experience and recapture the sense of loss which was originally traumatic; too unbearable to tolerate. She tries to re-create the experience in as colourful and dramatic a way as possible and believes that this helps the child to understand and master early terrors and trauma. In this session, we see her expressing on behalf of the child, an idea of a catastrophic loss which is echoed in Peter's comment about falling for ever. Peter indicates his interest in holes, looking at the gap in his teeth, while Tustin seems to be trying to fill the gap in his experience with her reconstructions of what she thinks it was that happened, to produce his trauma. She assumes that Peter is taking in what she has to say and that he is able to relate this to his own experience. In a way, she seems to be 'teaching him to grow', rather like the way he proposes to deal with his teeth!

Some of Peter's trauma may be sensed vicariously in this way, and marked improvements can be achieved in psychotherapy on the basis of identification with the therapist. In contrast, the experience of integration is always turbulent and the emotional cost is high. Peter's progress seems to have proceeded relatively smoothly, avoiding the upheavals of close contact with his emotional life. Some of Tustin's treatment records of this case, to which I have been privileged to have access, show clear hints of the beginnings of open hostility and resistance. Had she had sufficient time with this child, the emotional climate might have changed dramatically.

Peter achieves some mental development in this way, but with severe limitations. If he does not have the emotional experience to learn from, he cannot develop a capacity to think. Knowledge can continue to grow and seems to do so, by 'agglomeration' (Bion 1962a), but this is not to be confused with thinking or understanding. There is much evidence of his expanding knowledge which he likes to display to his therapist. We have yet to see, however, whether he will be able to achieve the emotional growth which his mother sought in bringing him to psychotherapy. Two brief extracts from the second year of treatment are added below to illustrate the potential for the emotional confrontation which is always necessary, if a real change of vertex and insight is to be achieved.

ONE YEAR ON

One year on from the first significant shift of focus, from his own keys to the therapist's possessions, another published session shows Peter reviewing his work with Tustin. Peter begins this session with an airy dismissal of Tustin's comments about an imminent break in therapy, while his parents are to be abroad. He tosses aside any idea of missing them and she openly suggests to him that he will miss his parents and his time with her. He follows this with a note of contempt as he recites to her Lewis Carroll's parody:

Twinkle, twinkle, little bat!
How I wonder what you're at!
Up above the world you fly!
Like a teatray in the sky.

Reminding him of the original version of the poem, together with previously expressed interests in *Jesus Christ Superstar*, Tustin gathers together his omnipotence, his superiority and his attack on feelings of dependence on an object. She interprets his illusory fusion with and control of the object which then turns to mockery and contempt when this illusion is challenged. His response following her interpretation is to smudge one of his drawings. 'Just a smear,' he says, before turning defensively to an obsessive checking and counting of his pictures, in much the same way as he had been checking his keys when he entered therapy (Tustin 1981a: 225). This is an illuminating moment which draws attention to the obsessional defences which come into play at this point and, continuing the rigid barrier between feelings and sensations, are the legacy of autistic anxieties.

In the same session, Peter goes on to present his therapist with the primitivity of his world. From the beginning of therapy, he had shown his fear of a toy crocodile which he associated with biting attacks and he had kept trying to hide it away in the playroom. Finally, it seems, he was so successful that the crocodile could not be found at all and Tustin had to supply a new one. On the day when the crocodile was replaced, Peter rediscovers a large pillar of Plasticine which also seems to have been secreted away inside another empty and unlocked drawer. It was a large conglomerate of all the different colours he had been given and it was out of this that he fashioned his god.

Peter has been concealing other resources too, it would seem, for in this session we also see him writing in sentences, he who, only a year ago, was described as merely holding a pencil. Now he writes, 'Do not touch the crocodile. It will eat you up' (Tustin 1981a: 229).

Peter's construction begins with the relationship between the family of dolls and this crocodile. The family has to be protected from biting attacks, so he wraps the crocodile up and places it in the bottom of his toy container with a cardboard floor on top. The crocodile is in prison, he says. Above, standing on this floor, he puts the doll family. After this he takes the block of Plasticine and, etching a face on it with his

GOD
AND
THE GUARD

THE FAMILY

THE CROCODILE.

Figure 2 Peter's construction of his 'world'

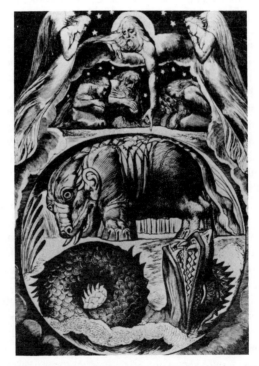

Figure 3 'Behemoth and Leviathan', engraving by William Blake

fingernail, says, 'That's God.' To Tustin's question, 'Does God take care of you?' he replies, 'No. I take care of him,' and adds, 'Then he takes care of me.' At this point, Peter breaks a piece off the body of God to make a guard. Covering over the family, he says it is now dark and the family is going to sleep. The crocodile is imprisoned below and God and his Guard stand above (Fig. 2).

Tustin likens the topography of Peter's construction to Blake's engraving (Fig. 3), where there is a similar disposition of objects: the dragon below, God and his angels above with the middle ground occupied by a singular creature with human ears. She sees Peter's 'world', like Blake's, as depicting the conflict of good and evil and the formation of a space between; a 'transitional' space, she says, 'where ordinary humanness seems to be coming into focus, to offset the polarities of bestiality and hyperspirituality' (ibid.: 229).

To my mind, there is one significant difference between Peter's and Blake's representations which it is important not to lose. Blake's picture is overarched by the combined goodness and benignity of the figures above, as if the midwives for the developing humanity below, which is much as Tustin interpreted the two pictures in her session. Peter's family, on the other hand, inhabit a very unsafe world where even God has to be guarded. The priority is to ensure safety but in a world which has not been safely divided into good and evil, for God is not secure in his position and has to be guarded.

Vigilance is unceasing, a characteristic both of autism and of obsessionality, and is primarily carried out by the eyes. It is interesting that Blake emphasises the ears of his developing creature. In autism, this is the sensory modality most often ignored or excluded from experience but in normal development the ears have a vital function of perceptual correlation. Human maternal care is characterised by soothing behaviour and containment of the infantile anxiety and this is communicated predominantly by verbal expression and received by the infant's auditory perceptions. As I have suggested elsewhere, the coming together of visual and auditory stimuli may be crucial to the formation of the concept of a containing object (Spensley 1992). In Peter's world, the perception of a good object has not been safely established and life remains unpredictable and hazardous.

PREMATURE ENDING

Tustin's notes on her third year of treatment are filled with Peter's conversations about words and ideas he has heard of. He asks her frequently whether she knows what certain words mean or he asks questions to which the answers seem obvious. Tustin meets this behaviour by showing him how he is treating her like a vending machine, as if his questions were like coins which he could use to get an expected response (Tustin 1981). The unexpected response from her could, on the other hand, produce a reaction of anger and fury which made it clear how much he resisted learning something new. His anger is expressed in confused ways, sometimes in self-attack when he bites his own hand, at another time by dropping a toy and 'making it hurt', but in this second year he also comes to making verbal attacks on Tustin too. He is rivalrous with her, constantly striving to show how he is bigger and better and knows more than she does, but he does so in a way which charms her.

By the end of this year, Peter's parents are also focussing on what he 'knows'. Peter is doing well enough at school for his parents to start thinking that he can relinquish some of his sessions. Since his educational progress has been good, they suggest that he should come fortnightly instead of weekly so as to spare them so much travel. This is tried for a time before another idea is launched which makes it impossible to continue. Mother has the notion that it would be better to move house to an area where Peter's past is unknown and he would be free of any stigma attached to his early disturbance. She feels that his oddness might not be noticed by strangers and that he could, as it were, start with a clean slate.

FOLLOW UP

Peter's family is one of the few who have kept in touch with Tustin, and she learned that they finally decided to go and live abroad where Peter could go to school, unknown, and free, they thought, of what they saw as the stigma of his autism. He seems to have continued to do quite well in academic work and wrote to Tustin at the time of his graduation from High School. His letter spoke cheerfully of 'the myriad number of subjects' he studied and of the trials of school assignments and of making money in holiday jobs. He was expecting to go on to college to major in biology. While he makes special mention of how well his sister is doing, his account of his own interests focusses on his concerns about the relative pay rates of his summer jobs, and the expenses of running his car.

He mentions his continuing proneness to angry outbursts, but does not seem greatly perturbed by this. 'Although I still get out of control when I am angry, family life has been going very nicely.' Peter is very impressed by Tustin's reputation and asks to be sent a copy of any new book she publishes. He promises to visit when he returns to England but, rather naively, seems to assume that he will be able to see her conducting a session.

This quality of concreteness became more apparent to Tustin when Peter did finally come to visit her after his graduation from college and told her about some of his career thoughts. He was then in his early twenties and somewhat obese but greeted her with politeness and charm. He assured her again that he was very happy for his treatment material to be used for publication in the interests of being helpful to other children.

There had been a number of career options in his mind; a somewhat strange assortment of alternatives which raised questions about what it was that he was seeking from his career. His first choice was to become a Buddhist but he was not accepted. Next, he tried a physiotherapy training, but he had had to give that up when it was considered that he lacked adequate emotional contact with his clients.

When he came to see Tustin, he was full of thoughts of becoming an osteopath and she, with characteristic generosity, took him to see a nearby practitioner whom she knew. She noticed, however, that Peter seemed less interested in what the osteopath had to say about the profession, than in looking around at the things he could see in the treatment room. He had a delightfully friendly manner but Tustin was left with a distinct impression of his personal and emotional insularity.

Peter was slow to settle down into meaningful work but finally turned to computers. From his mother, Tustin later learnt that he had joined a very strict religious sect within which, she believed, the life of religious ritual would help to hold him together. He had returned to his family roots and traditions. It was even possible that a marriage would be arranged for him within this community.

Peter's story is one of continuing struggle to find emotional meaningfulness in life and Tustin saw him as brave and courageous in the face of overwhelming odds. He has come a long way from the mute and withdrawn state which had impressed Bergman and caused his parents to have him investigated for deafness. He functions well in practical ways, and he appreciates the commercial realities of life, but the difficulties of personal relationships which concerned his mother when he was six years old remain a problem. His insensitivity to people was apparent to his physiotherapy supervisors and Tustin too experienced a certain immaturity and inappropriateness in his social contact and manner. Peter recognises threats to his self-control at times and Mother echoes this when she talks of his need to find something 'to hold him together'. In the absence of a secure sense of emotional containment, Peter's attachments are thin and in Meltzer's terms 'adhesive'. He is object-seeking, but there is little empathy with the object and therefore little depth to his relationships. We see him trying to make the most of the opportunities he can find to foster his human contacts and in this the ritual and supports of religious life are not to be despised.

Chapter 10

Mental handicap and mental illness

The only feature common to all mental disorders is the loss of common sense (sensus communis) *and the compensatory development of a unique sense* (sensus privatus) *of reasoning.*
Immanuel Kant, *The Classification of Mental Diseases* (1798)

THE IMPAIRED MIND

In other chapters I have referred to the history of psychiatry and to the growing interest in understanding whether any meaningfulness lay hidden behind the phenomena of the different forms of mental disease. Today, the Mental Health Act (1983) makes provision for the care and treatment of 'mentally disordered' patients and goes on to specify and differentiate within this broad range certain categories of mental disorder. In particular, mental *impairment* – for 'handicap' is now an outdated and an outmoded term – is distinguished from mental illness and defined as 'a state of arrested or incomplete development of mind'. The Act includes among the criteria for mental impairment, a significant impairment of intelligence. Level of intelligence, an important and critical distinction, is also the most readily quantifiable characteristic, with the result that intellectual retardation has tended in practice to become the definitive criterion, notwithstanding the recognition and acceptance of the variety of aetiologies. Thus the cognitive characteristics and the phenomena of learning impairment are to be found in a wide range of conditions, physical, psychological, constitutional and genetic.

The highlighting of the cognitive features in this way, together with the growth of cognitive psychology as a whole, has emphasised the differences between mental impairment and mental illness, the latter associated predominantly with emotional factors. The International

Classification of Diseases recognises that mental retardation often involves psychiatric disturbance but recommends that such features be coded separately to indicate an *associated* condition. In this way, mental disorder has been deeply split into two diagnostic categories seen to have very different aetiologies and prognoses (Spensley 1985b).

Personality disturbance, now widely associated with emotional determinants, has long been accepted as the basis of psychiatric illness, and contrasts with traditional views about mental impairment where, in addition to the known organic conditions, a concept of deficit has prevailed, in particular, a deficit of cognitive ability with implications here too of organic origins. Until the discovery of autism by Kanner in 1943, there was little cross fertilisation of ideas between the two major fields of mental disorder. In accordance with psychology's long-standing tripartite division of the human mind into cognitive, conative and affective components, mental illness has been seen as an affective disorder and mental impairment as a disorder of cognition.

The division and separation of mental disorder into psychiatric illness and mental impairment has encouraged the tendency to treat the designation mental impairment as if it were a diagnostic entity, some-what akin to the use of the term idiocy in the nineteenth century. Mild, moderate, severe, or profound impairment, determined by intellectual testing, is a form of classification which tells us only of the degree of learning disablement and disregards indicators of aetiology, the nature of the impairment or of the residual potential for psychical growth.

The progression of changes in nomenclature, from nineteenth-century imbecility and idiocy through terms of subnormality and defi-ciency to today's 'learning difficulty', is the indication of an increasing diagnostic sophistication and represents a gradual but significant recog-nition of (a) the centrality of the learning processes to human develop-ment and (b) of impediments to learning rather than defects. Similarities of mental functioning between the learning-disabled and the psychotic arise from the characteristics of psychological projection and evacua-tion which they have in common and which so devastate the capacity to integrate and to learn. The breeding ground of these primitive processes, as Bion has shown (Bion 1962a, b), lies in an inability to tolerate frustration, for whatever reason, and it is not surprising that this should include physical impairments as *agents provocateurs*. Intolerable levels of frustration, which intrude upon the natural course of psychic develop-ment, may arise from a range of sources – emotional, environmental, physical or organic.

EDUCATING THE LEARNING-DISABLED

Special education for the mentally handicapped, or indeed for any handicapped children in this country, is of relatively recent origin. The first specific provision was the Asylum for Idiots, established in Highgate in 1847, and until the Education (Handicapped Children) Act 1970 responsibility for the educational future of children with learning difficulties was in the hands of Health Authorities, not Education. It was a medical officer who would determine whether a particular child should be educated in an ordinary school, a special school, or not at all. Before 1970, the level of provision for the learning impaired varied throughout the country and the emphasis was usually more on training than education. Those who responded to guidance and training grew up able to perform simple tasks and to take responsibility for manual duties, most commonly of a domestic or agricultural nature.

After 1970, a new perspective on the mentally handicapped meant that they were no longer to be regarded as educationally sub-normal or ineducable but as educationally disabled and all children, however serious their disability, were to be included within the ambit of special education. The Warnock Report (1978), seeking to dispel any stigma associated with impairment, recommended the use of the description 'children with learning difficulties' and stressed their special educational needs rather than disabilities. The report acknowledged the new need for specialist training for the teachers of this very disadvantaged group of children, but the problems of how the 'ineducable' were now to be educated remained.

A rapid programme of expansion of educational provision was set in train and specially equipped schools were established throughout the country. The nation's response had been motivated mostly by general feelings of guilt about a section of the child population whose rights had been neglected. The nature of the impairments to the learning processes that had led to some children's being regarded as ineducable and the specificity of the 'educational' needs that now had to be met were left largely unexplored. Teachers trained for mainstream education were now faced with a most daunting problem and, despite the recommendations for specialist training, much had to be learned on the job, and teachers undertaking this new task have been exposed to high levels of frustration and despair.

Autistic children, once numbered among the mentally handicapped and not differentiated from them, now attract special educational attention. Another result of Kanner's discoveries has been the subsequent recognition of residual 'autistic features' in a significant number of other groups of the mentally impaired, not diagnosed as autistic. This means that what has been learned from the study of autism is by no means limited to those with 'classical' symptoms and much of the understanding gained from the study of autism has a direct relevance to the kinds of difficulties met with among the mentally impaired in general.

Our attitudes to the mentally impaired have become much more sophisticated and civilised but it is important that the enthusiasms of empathy or political zeal on behalf of an undervalued group do not obscure the extent of the psychological impoverishment intrinsic to the condition. Whilst similarities in behaviour and, perhaps, experience between the mentally ill and the mentally impaired are of major interest and relevance to the treatment and 'education' of the latter, the essential differences between the two groups remain and must not be minimised if help is to be appropriate and meaningful. Impairment in the capacity to learn, by definition, seriously delimits treatability.

Those teachers, nurses and welfare workers in close everyday contact with the mentally impaired, particularly in residential institutions, are charged with a formidable task. In trying to find ways to encourage optimal development, they have a responsibility placed upon them for facilitating and managing the lives of those with whom all others before them have felt helpless to cope. There are few rewards, and the work is likely to tax the most equable of temperaments. Difficulties in learning and receptivity are endemic but no such obstruction is experienced in relation to expressive behaviour and aggression. Care staff are always at the receiving end of the action and readily become focal points of hostility; not only that of the children or clients in their care, but also of relatives, quick to attribute criticism and to complain of failures in the staff to produce results.

The introduction of psychodynamically informed approaches to management in such settings can bring considerable relief to teaching and care staff. The dynamics which have to be understood are those which characterise autism, not those of inter-personal conflict, and it is here that Tustin's delineation of the entangled and encapsulated forms of disturbance has been so helpful. To understand that disturbed behaviour can be related to primitive terror and does not necessarily have to be directly linked with an externally precipitating factor opens up a new range of responses. I shall have more to say of this approach to the management of the mentally impaired in the next chapter.

The majority of those once deemed ineducable remain so, for many suffer intractable organic deformation and damage and many have little or no language. This does not mean, however, that nothing can appropriately be offered to encourage optimal development. For some, custodial and nursing care may still be the most that can appropriately be offered, even in an environment which is intended for cognitive stimulation and growth, as I had to assure one teacher, feeling guilty about how little she could do for a severely and multiply disabled boy of eight.

RODDY

Roddy lived with his schizophrenic mother and was brought to school each day by school minibus. The boy hardly communicated, and his body, thin and stiff as a board, lay rigidly in his wheelchair until someone moved him. Concerned particularly about the stiffness of the child's body and because he often seemed unwashed when he arrived from home, the teacher began to give him baths. Her uneasy feeling that this was not a legitimate part of her duties as a teacher was offset by her conviction that bathing was about the only activity which evoked a response from Roddy. These sensory experiences brought the only indications of pleasurable feeling and the warm water also seemed to restore a slight degree of flexibility to his limbs. Her considerable patience and sensitivity were occasionally rewarded by a weak smile.

I was present at one of these bathing sessions on a day when Roddy appeared unable to make any response at all and we could only guess at making him comfortable. That afternoon, he went home as usual, in the minibus, but the next day news came that he had died. On my following visit to the school, I found the teacher even more doubtful about her activities. Had she been causing distress rather than giving relief in his last hours of life? It was hard to be sure of the answer to that question, but it seemed to me that her common-sense attitude and tender physical care were more likely than not to have provided some sense of comfort and solace.

An extreme example, to be sure, but there are many very severely disabled children attending special schools for the learning-disabled, where the primary need is for good physical care. This, in itself, needs to be valued as an important carrier of psychological benefit, just as the mother's physical ministrations do in the early weeks of infant life. Tustin's work in autism has also alerted us to the primitive significance of early sensory experience and its part in the learning processes. Her findings are no less pertinent to the forms of mental impairment other than those due to autism.

I quote the case of Roddy to emphasise how much, for children at this extreme of disability, 'education' calls more for nursing and therapeutic skills than for teaching. Teachers and care workers, bedevilled by anxieties that there is some 'higher' psychological skill which they do not possess, frequently devalue the common-sense work they already do. Care staff also need clinical support to be able to accept that the legitimate needs and anxieties of a hefty teenager with severe learning disablement may be closer to those of an infant than to his peers. In such cases, practices and policies which urge 'normalisation' can create bewilderment and intensify withdrawal rather than provide a stimulus to development.

Approaches which stress 'normalisation', and equality of provision for the mentally impaired, can even, unwittingly, do a disservice. Holidays, parties, shopping trips, all seen as part of a right to enjoy the same amenities as normal children, are experienced by some of the mentally impaired, not as a treat but as a nightmare. Outings, like the seaside holiday, can be extremely confusing and disturbing for many mentally impaired children, for whom the possibility of enjoyment is obliterated by their fears of change and of the unfamiliar. At times holidays have to be abandoned for some children because of their alarm and disturbance. Even so, it is hard to get away from convictions that such treats ought to be enjoyed and that the way to improve and broaden the lives of the mentally impaired is to introduce as many 'normal' pursuits as possible into their lives. Such thinking takes little account of the fact that the experience of the mentally impaired is likely to be very different because of that impairment. Not having a seaside holiday, for example, can be a blessed relief not a deprivation.

When we dare to admit such observations, opportunities open for the consideration of more appropriate uses of the available resources. This would imply closer research to ascertain needs in the light of increasing psychological knowledge of primitive anxiety states. Improvements in the level of training and support available to care staff are also a priority deserving urgent attention.

PSYCHOTHERAPY AND THE LEARNING-DISABLED

Like education, psychotherapy for the mentally impaired had long been regarded as inappropriate and, like education, it is important now to examine what, if any, relevance psychoanalytic knowledge has for the understanding of the problems of the functionally and organically impaired. Already some psychotherapists have been exploring the application of individual psychotherapy to mentally impaired, learning-disabled children and adults (Alvarez 1980, Symington 1981, Spensley 1985a, b, Balbirnie 1985, Sinason 1986, 1992), but the theoretical implications of using an insight-led approach to the problems created by learning (and insight) disability have yet to be fully examined and understood.

Failure to learn is inevitably accompanied by failure to comprehend personal relationships which means that both the starting point and the course of psychotherapy will be problematic. Alvarez (1992) has given a detailed and moving account of the slow, arduous struggle to reach the dawn of comprehension. Just as Tustin (and Alvarez) cautions against the transposing of therapeutic techniques suited to neurotic and border-line patients to the treatment of autism and psychosis, so must we be equally cautious about the suitability of treatment approaches to the mentally impaired whose conditions, with different aetiologies, include psychotic impairments in their capacity to comprehend mental space, i.e. to 'mentalise'.

This century's two most significant and influential developments in the theory of mental disorder have come from the studies of Kanner and Bion and it is befitting that one has emerged from work in the mental handicap environment and the other from the arena of mental illness. These contributions complement one another, with results which con-tinue to influence the basis of our thinking about all mental disorder. Kanner discovered that in the midst of the severest cognitive impair-ment, affective factors had to be taken into account, while Bion intro-duced new and radical ideas about the processes of human thinking, arguing that emotional growth both preceded and provided the basis for cognitive development.

In the field of mental impairment these advances in thinking were followed by a surge of interest in establishing a specifically cognitive deficit, fortifying the differences and re-establishing the gulf between emo-tional and cognitive factors in mental development. Research in autism moved away from Kanner's first interest in affective factors (Rutter 1983) and in Britain autism was to remain predominantly in the domain of learning disability along with those learning disabilities of established organic origin. In the United States, the concept of deficit emerged afresh, however, this time in the context of mental illness. Kohut advocated a concept of emotional deficit (Kohut 1985), seeing psychoanalysis now as a task of emotional restoration more than the classical Freudian aim of resolving conflict. Kohut's ideas are consistent with the psychoanalytic understanding of autism but such links have not been developed.

Concepts of deficit readily come to the minds of those attempting to communicate with the mentally disordered, whether they are diagnosed mentally impaired or mentally ill. Popular 'diagnoses' like 'not all there', 'not the full shilling', 'a screw loose', all convey a commonly held perception that the core of the difficulties is a mental deficit. The use of such a concept is not inappropriate, but professional opinions differ widely in their conceptualisations of deficiency and its causative factors.

A 'mental' impairment, whether it be organically or emotionally engendered, always means the loss of a capacity to symbolise and think one's thoughts. Even when there is good verbal ability, there is a world of difference between the patient who, without the mental space for symbol formation, views himself as an object to be given things in concrete ways – and this includes verbal help, advice, recommendations, etc. – and the patient who can feel some responsibility for his needs, his feelings, his thoughts and his behaviour and thinks of himself, therefore, as a subject. A subject not only feels responsible for his own life but can appreciate his objects (in the Kleinian sense) as being subjects in their own right. The unfortunate who is stuck in a concrete world of objects, unable to feel the experience of a mental dimension to life, is imprisoned in this very restricted *sensus privatus*. This is a world of events which lack both the experience of thoughts and feelings (neither his own nor those of others) and the 'common' sense necessary for communication and learning. Bion has pointed out that the verbal patient in so primitive a state of mind is not employing articulate speech in the service of communication, but is instead, 'demonstrating with evident sincerity an inability to understand his own state of mind, even when it is pointed out to him' (Bion 1962b). No more accurate or penetrating assessment could be offered of my experience with Sam, whose predicament is described below.

From the case loads of social workers, the patients most frequently brought to me for consultation at the Willesden Centre for Psychological Treatment come into this category, their diagnoses considered to lie somewhere between mental impairment and personality disorder. These are usually importunate personalities with good verbal abilities, who pester the social worker with repeated requests for support of their ideas and wishes, yet never derive any satisfaction from the many provisions and opportunities arranged for them. Often referred to as mildly mentally impaired because of their learning difficulties, they can be considered, because of their verbal fluency, to be suitable for and interested in psychotherapy – a talking treatment! The psychotherapist then discovers that what she has to offer the patient is treated in the same manner and suffers a fate similar to that of all the social worker's attempts to be helpful.

SAM WANTS A GIRL

Sam had been referred because of repeated problems in the group home where he lived with a number of other people having social difficulties. He had a modest job in a warehouse which he had been able to hold for some time with the help of employers who accepted him as a disabled person and made allowances for his occasional bad-tempered outbursts. Mostly, he would get along well enough, supported both in the job and by the provisions of his group home, but there was growing unease about his aggressive jealousy which broke out in both environments from time to time when Sam began to feel discontented and unsettled. His complaints were always about his dissatisfaction that he did not have friends or that people were not friendly towards him, so it was thought that he might benefit from an opportunity to talk about and to understand more about himself and the resentment which made him want to attack others.

When I talked to Sam, I found him well able to give me a coherent account of his complaints and a clear indication of what he thought he needed and wanted. He did get angry with certain people at times, he said, but he always thought that he had been provoked unnecessarily. It angered him that others seemed to be able to do things he was excluded from and he did not see why he should be left out. He made particular mention of his wish to have a girl-friend. Others at the group home had girl-friends and they could go for walks together or sit down and watch the television together. He thought that would be nice and he did not see why he should not also have someone like that for himself. One of the rows at the group home had been caused by his attempt to take over someone else's girl and at work there had been complaints that he was, inappropriately, approaching and touching the girls there.

I talked with Sam about his loneliness and how he wanted just to be able to be given a girl-friend, like he might be given a present. He agreed, but the trouble was that he saw nothing inappropriate about this wish. From my sessions with him, I could only conclude that he had no awareness of and no interest in his feelings. He ignored any reference to loneliness, jealousy, or resentment, as if feelings had no meaning. They were experienced concretely as things in themselves and not as phenomena representative of a state of mind. If anger and aggression were to be got rid of, then he must have that which would remove his resentment. If he had a girl companion, he argued, he would not have the anger or the resentment. In this way access to the feelings which might have offered routes to insight was firmly sealed off. Without insight there was little possibility of a change of attitude which could result in a change of behaviour to make *him* a more accepting and a more acceptable companion. He had no thoughts about the relationship he might have with a girl. It was as if he saw her as a living doll who would replace the painful gap in his life. For Sam it was a simple and obvious equation. Words for Sam were closer to actions than thought.

The impression I gained from my interviews with this man was further supported by his history. I found that he had already had three years of psychotherapy, but all he could say about that was that it didn't seem to have been much good because he still did not have a girl-friend! He did not remember the name of his previous psychotherapist, but he was still interested in talking to anyone about getting a girl-friend. This young man was demonstrating how he had not been able to learn in the past and how he continued not to be able to learn, because he did not have an awareness of the emotional experience from which he might begin to learn. Not being able to learn from experience because of the lack of that experience constitutes a very serious deficit. The approach to psychotherapy in such cases has much in common with the specific difficulties encountered in the treatment of autism and is an equally formidable undertaking. Sam's dilemma can be compared with that of Tustin's patient Peter, for whom personal emotional relationships remained of limited interest, despite his educational achievements.

SARAH SEEKS A HOME

A social worker's problem with Sarah was brought to me for consultation when she was beginning to suspect that her work with her client was ineffectual and that she was getting drawn into a repetitious pattern of short-term relief followed by renewed dissatisfaction. Sarah was convinced that she would be happy and settled if she lived in the right environment but her quest to find the right environment was becoming costly as well as frustrating, and her social worker was now torn between her sympathy for and wish to help Sarah and her own common-sense perception that Sarah's adamant beliefs about what she needed were mistaken.

Sarah had spent most of her early life in London in unhappy and unstable circumstances. Her mother had been unable to care for her properly and she was moved to relatives and then into institutional care and for part of that period lived in foster care. Her school attainment was poor and she was considered backward and eventually placed in special schooling, which she saw as unfair and stigmatising. Acknowledging specific difficulties in reading and arithmetic, she nevertheless saw herself as equal in intelligence to her peer group and nowadays often thinks herself superior in ability to many of her companions who had not been relegated to 'special' schools in their childhood. Though importunate in her needs for attention, she is now a friendly, personable individual with a talkative nature. It is this verbal fluency and her outspokenness which, as in Sam's case, tends to obscure the impairment in thinking capacities and leads to her views of herself being treated as insightful and her suggestions realistic.

Sarah was able to live a relatively independent life within her group home and she regarded herself, as did many of the staff, as one of the more successful residents. As a result it was assumed that she had the potential to attain greater independence and care staff were therefore particularly sympathetic to her own ideas for such advances. She talked a lot about a memory from her chequered early life, a time when she had felt particularly happy when she went to live with an aunt in Devon. She had spent two years there from about the age of eight and this experience, referred to only as 'when I was in Devon', began to take on more and more significance as the place where she would really be happy and contented. Despite some professional reservations, it was finally agreed that she should go, and the complex official arrangements were undertaken to transfer her care from a London Social Work Department to another in Devon. All of this work was carried out in an atmosphere of co-operation and understanding. Sarah went to Devon and settled into her new life – but not for long.

About a year later she began to feel depressed and unhappy again and said she had made a great mistake in coming to Devon. She said she had not appreciated that her memories belonged to the past and she was finding that she was not making the friends in the present and not finding the contentment she had dreamed of. Could she return to London, a much more familiar place where she now appreciated all her friends and companions to be?

The rearrangement was a bit tiresome but social workers involved were still sympathetic, appreciating her disappointment but impressed by her attempts at finding a congenial environment and by an apparent reflectiveness in her about her actions and reactions. It was several months after the second transfer had been completed when she began again to talk of having misjudged the situation and was filled with renewed confidence that Devon really would be the right place for her after all. Her social worker then contacted me to explore the case. She did not want to investigate any further moves until she had had an opportunity to think about what was happening. Anyway, she suspected the sympathies of the Local Authorities involved might now be wearing rather thin.

In my discussions with the social worker, it was a relief to her to hear that I viewed the problem as deep and largely intractable. Her own common sense had been leading her to the same conclusion, but she had felt guilty about this on two counts. One, that she would be letting her client down if she did not once again try to support what appeared to be positive wishes for independent living, and the other that she should be able to demonstrate a success with a client like Sarah who gave the impression of being articulate and insightful. Like Sam, however, Sarah could only treat her needs concretely, so that with every dissatisfaction a move and a change of circumstances were believed to be the solution. While the social worker could use her common sense to see that this was proving hollow, her client could not.

The social worker, with the mental space to process or 'digest' the experience, could allow a new perspective and new thoughts on the problem to emerge in her mind. Her client, in the absence of that mental space, could not. Her experience remained undigested and suited only for projection or evacuation or storage as undigested facts (Bion 1962b). As a result, both Sam and Sarah, like many of those with so-called 'mild' learning disability, had a fund of undigested emotional 'facts' to talk about, but this was not to be confused with insight and thinking. Their learning disability is very far from 'mild' but it is more helpful to them that this be recognised than that their problems be magnified by the pressures of unrealistic expectations on both client and worker.

These cases highlight a central confusion which arises from the inherent pathology at this level of functional disturbance – the difference between can't and won't, which it is essential to distinguish. Impairments in thinking and learning arise from the absence of the experience vital to those processes, however that lack has been brought about. When the patient because of this lack of experience cannot differentiate between 'can't' and 'won't', it is vital that the worker does, if the patient is to be helped. Collusion on this critical issue results in the perpetuation of fruitless action in the external world in pursuit of a change which is required internally.

RUBY

An agoraphobic child of fifteen once caused me to give rigorous thought to the meaning of mental impairment and the difference between 'won't' and 'can't'. She had to be brought to treatment by her mother in a taxi because she could not travel by public transport and there were similar difficulties in her getting to school. The school was co-operative and sympathetic and the head teacher went to considerable lengths to provide conditions in which the girl might continue to work for her O-level examinations. She offered her own room as a 'bolt hole' for Ruby whenever she was seized by panic and a desperate urgency to get out of the classroom and she saw Ruby as in need of additional support to build her confidence. As part of this, she wrote to me to request that I support her application to the local council for taxi expenses for Ruby, on the grounds that she could not use public transport to get to school.

As her psychotherapist, I did not want to contaminate my psycho-therapeutic relationship with my patient by becoming associated with this application but I was also concerned how to explain my position to the teacher and to Ruby's mother, both of whom saw the need as urgent and the request as fully justified. My co-operation in the authorisation was taken for granted, and expected to be a simple formality. I did not think it would be easy for them to appreciate the reasons for my reservations but I felt sure that it would be detrimental to Ruby's therapy for me to be drawn into action of this kind. The situation demanded that I formulate a clear account of my position and the need which I saw to protect the psychotherapeutic work which could be conveyed in a way which would be comprehensible to Ruby, her mother and the headmistress.

The justification for the taxi service rested on the assumption that Ruby could not use public transport. She would panic to such an extent that nothing could persuade her to get on a bus or a train even when accompanied, so it seemed self-evident that she could not travel to school that way. The only alternative was a car, and since her widowed mother did not possess one the taxi was a necessity and her approaching O-levels made the matter even more urgent.

It was only when I noticed the confusion between 'won't' and 'can't' that I found a way through this logical impasse. I accepted that Ruby did not travel by public transport but said that I did not accept that she *could not.* My argument was that she might believe that she *could not,* but that if we were to behave as if we believed the same, we would be colluding with her delusion and undermining her tenuous hold on reality. She was a healthy young girl, not disabled, except by her beliefs about herself which required to be challenged not accepted by those whose grasp of reality and common sense was stronger. The validity of my argument was gracefully accepted by all and my therapeutic position remained intact.

I do not recall whether the taxi was ultimately procured by other means or not. However, when in due course Ruby lost her symptoms, her reaction was striking. Her mother was delighted by her recovery, but Ruby was utterly contemptuous of the help she had received. 'Anyone can get on a train. People do that every day. What is so special about that?' was her retort, full of resentment about having to recognise that she had needed help with an ordinary everyday matter and that she had been so overwhelmed by anxiety that her perception of 'can't' and 'won't' had been distorted.

Ruby was mentally ill, not mentally impaired, and her symptom presents a different perspective on the can't/won't confusion. In the case of Sam and Sarah, their serious inabilities, their 'deficit', their 'can't', was concealed and mistaken for 'won't'. It was assumed, for example, that their understanding of companionship was the same as the therapist's, and this led to the consequent incomprehension, insatiability and impasse in the psychotherapeutic endeavour to be of help. Ruby, on the other hand, claimed 'can't' to disguise a pathological 'won't' and this had to be recognised and challenged if the perpetuation of her symptom were not to be colluded with. In the case of the mentally impaired it is vital to appreciate the extent of the autistic failure to comprehend the therapeutic object and the therapeutic objective because of the 'black hole' in their emotional experience which leaves them unable to learn.

Chapter 11

Psychoanalytic perspectives on learning impairment

Reason is emotion's slave, and exists to rationalise emotional experience.

Bion (1970)

The qualifications I have been expressing in the last chapter are not to suggest that I consider psychoanalytic knowledge to have little to contribute to the problems of the mentally impaired. On the contrary, the Workshop at the Willesden Centre for Psychological Treatment exists to introduce a psychoanalytic perspective into the work of psychologists working in the field of mental impairment. The Workshop for Development and Research in Psychoanalytic Applications to Learning Impairment was made possible by the support of a generous grant from the Maurice Laing Foundation. Its meetings are attended in the main by psychologists in the London area, but its approach has interested psychologists (and psychiatrists) from other parts of Britain and from abroad. Galloway, a member of the workshop, reports some encouraging results in the containment of violent behaviour at Kingsbury Hospital, where, in the special unit for Challenging Behaviour, psychoanalytic concepts inform the management regime (Galloway 1993, Cooray 1993).

The benefits of psychoanalytic understanding are not exclusive to the intelligent and sensitive, to that sector of society which, in America, was given the cynical acronym YAVIS (Young, Affluent, Verbal, Intelligent, and Sensitive). It is in our institutions, particularly in the case of the learning-impaired, that disturbed primitive behaviour is most in evidence and it is there that the understanding of unconscious impulses and behaviour are most needed and where inadequate understanding or misunderstanding can have significant implications, sometimes with catastrophic consequences. For example, the misattribution of meaning and motivation where none exists may lead to measures which can all too easily end in an escalation of tension, fear and violence. Here Tustin's work, in illuminating the primitive depth of behaviours which had previously appeared to be inexplicable, offers the possibility of seeing alternative ways of making sense of the kind of behaviour which was either given arbitrary meaning or was regarded as meaningless.

Management of disturbed behaviour which is not psychodynamically informed is not only greatly weakened but can even unwittingly increase the problems. Everyday methods of discipline, which carry the assumption of some degree of self-control in the client, can constitute the final straw for those who are already struggling to hold themselves together. When panic and terror threaten to overwhelm and cannot be contained any longer, explosive rage is the final defence. To attempt to control this with any form of management which presupposes a capacity for self-control not only brings frustration and failure, but is likely to increase rather than decrease rage and violence.

This telling anecdote well illustrates the dilemma. A deeply disturbed obsessional compulsive lady was struggling to return home from abroad at the height of her obsessionality. Although she would not have been numbered among the learning-disabled, her capacity to use her high intelligence was severely impaired by mental illness. Checking of all her actions had reached almost unmanageable proportions. She had taken days to get packed but her appearance and behaviour raised the suspicions of customs officers and she was asked at the airport to open up her luggage for search. At first, she tried to explain her predicament and how she felt she could not possibly comply, because it would take her days to repack and her flight plans would be totally destroyed. When the officers, naturally, insisted and began to unpack her things, regardless, she became utterly desperate, attacked a female customs officer and ended up in prison!

The customs officers, carrying out their duties as usual, were not to know that they were dealing with a woman who, at that moment, was so desperately anxious and mentally ill that she was quite incapable of the psychological containment of her terrors. To ask her to unpack all that she had finally and painfully managed to put together was, for her, tantamount to opening Pandora's Box. To act as if she were in control of herself and could differentiate sufficiently between phantasy and reality to be able to comply with instructions, resulted in an explosive attack on others but it was motivated by self-protection. Her already feeble hold on her self-control left no margin for her to be able to manage any additional anxiety. She was clinging precariously to a concrete form of 'containment' in the packed suitcases, feeling as if her life depended on the durability of that achievement.

In Britain, responsibility for training and treatment programmes for the learning-disabled is usually in the hands of clinical psychologists, who, for decades, have been developing and practising methods of teaching and training for the mentally impaired which have their rationale in learning theory and which place greatest emphasis on behaviour and how to shape and encourage social living. The objective of the Willesden Centre Workshop is not to supersede this approach, but to supplement it. Behavioural work has its own validity, and continues to be used and to be useful in this environment. Any management strategy which promotes order, routine and predictability cannot but be helpful in the unorganised and confusing world of the mentally impaired and needs to be valued, not deprecated, nor rejected as 'institutionalisation'.

THE CONTRIBUTIONS OF BEHAVIOURAL AND COGNITIVE PSYCHOLOGY

Management policies in relation to the learning-disabled are predominantly based, at present, on the principles of behavioural and cognitive psychology. Emphasis is placed on the encouragement of good and socially acceptable behaviour and on either ignoring or discouraging unacceptable behaviour. As I have already indicated, this is not to be despised, but its inadequacy to deal with entrenched and persistent behavioural disturbances, particularly the problems of violence, is a source of fatigue and stress in the carers and, as such, frequently gives cause for concern. It is also well established that the custodial care of the most impaired and disabled is most often in the hands of those with the least training.

Learning theory, rooted as it is in ideas of reinforcement of desired characteristics and extinction or attrition of the undesirable traits, requires a modicum of compliance and co-operation from the client or patient, and if this can be achieved progress can be made. All too often, however, the experience of the worker is to find cases where these techniques fail to make an impact and the consequence is for the worker to feel a sense of failure or hopelessness, or, worse, to feel desperate to gain control over the seemingly mindless and wanton destructiveness of some of the individuals in their care. An example of this gradual erosion of hope in relation to helping a desperate patient follows and will also serve to illustrate how a difference of approach to the problem can alter the response.

JOHN

John was thirteen years old when I first met him in a residential school for learning-disabled children and young people. He had been causing grave concern and anxiety to nursing and care staff because of his self-injurious behaviour. John was given to persistent outbursts of head punching which had continued over many years since childhood. His head and hair bore the signs of abuse where on one side of his head the bone structure was somewhat flattened and there was a patch where his hair grew sparsely. John had recently been moved from a large mental handicap hospital to the new educational provision and the staff at the new residence, deeply disturbed to discover how helpless they were in the face of John's persistent and aggressive attacks on himself, were beginning to despair of finding an effective way of controlling his outbursts of mindless violence.

I heard how they had tried everything. At first they attempted to distract him with other occupations, favourite foods, toys, or play activities, but to no avail. Next they tried restriction, holding the hand which he used to beat himself with, but then found that he would start to hit himself with his free hand, on the other side of his head. When two workers tried to restrain him, holding his hands, one on either side, he would make powerful efforts to butt his head against any reachable wall. The effort required to control him was exhausting and sometimes they resorted to sitting on his hands one on either side as they tried to interest him in the television.

John's behaviour was deeply disturbing to all observers, who would invariably feel driven to search for some way of stopping such cruelty. One day, I encountered John in the midst of one of his episodes, two exhausted and frustrated nurses by his side, trying to control his violent blows to his own head. As a witness to this, I, too, was filled with thoughts of how to stop him. Instinctively, as he rained blows on himself, I found myself putting my hands not on his hands but on his poor head. The result was dramatic when he stopped instantly, his battering hand suddenly arrested, poised in mid-air.

This is not to suggest a magical solution to the problem. John's disturbing behaviour had not been instantaneously eliminated. I cite this incident rather to exemplify the directional change of approach to a problem. A significant shift of emphasis becomes possible when sufficient containment of the anxiety aroused allows for something other than prevention or suppression to be considered. The approach to the problem from another angle brought a response suggesting that it was worthy of attention. Such a difference of approach is also illustrative of Bion's borrowing of the mathematical term 'vertex' to indicate the different configurations of a problem made possible with a shift of perspective or change of 'sense' or 'system' from which the problem is viewed (Bion 1965). Tustin has led the way in drawing attention to the hidden terrors which underlie mindless and seemingly meaningless destructiveness.

Among the most challenging and urgently presented problems which clinical psychologists are asked to help with in residences and institutions are those involving violence. Violence may be directed towards persons, property or, equally if not more disturbingly, as in John's case, it may be self-directed. Desperate individuals, particularly children, who use their bodies as battering-rams, can display an awesome and inhuman strength which is horrifying to the helpless onlooker and cries out only to be stopped, as the previous case illustrates. Where there is organic impairment, mindless violence may defy understanding, but its non-verbal impact on the carer remains powerful. The threat to the carer's mental balance is not to be underestimated and when the terrors of the patient get under the skins of the caretakers, the impulse to retaliate and 'beat' the mindlessness can escalate the violence. The occasional reported scandal bears witness to this.

THE PSYCHODYNAMICS OF VIOLENCE

An understanding of the dynamics of violence can go a long way towards helping to avert serious trouble. Training and management regimes which are psychodynamically informed provide carers with new and different approaches to their problems, ones which offer an alternative to crude methods of control and restraint. Tustin's work, particularly, has a direct application, insofar as she has tried to illuminate primitive pre-mental states which do not conform to the logic of common sense. These are the sensory-dominated states which Tustin has described as characteristic of autism, but they are not limited to autism. Similar states are common among those who suffer serious mental impairment with other aetiologies. The value of Tustin's work to the field of mental impairment is only beginning to be appreciated. Her intuitive thinking brings fresh interest and kindles new enthusiasms in an area long associated with the most difficult and intractable of therapeutic problems. There is reason to be hopeful that a more sophisticated understanding of what drives those with limited mental capacities will bring a more meaningful rationale to their care and guidance.

It is understandable that care staff should be concerned to mitigate and, if possible, pre-empt outbursts of violence but if such concerns concentrate on vigilance and strict supervision, the result can be to heighten tension and persecutory fears. It is also essential to ensure that fear in the carers is not added to a violent situation so as to increase the risk of eruption and loss of control. Terrorisers are always terrified people and nothing increases the risk of violence more than the sensing of fear in those who are expected to be in charge.

This is a difficult proposition for the psychologically unsophisticated, who are much more likely to assume intention, motivation and deviousness in the offender and to attribute to them responsibility and accountability for their actions. That a terroriser could, himself, be in fear for his life is usually greeted with incredulity. It seems unbelievable, because the threat to the aggressor is unseen and unreal to those who are threatened by him. Nevertheless, the unseen phantasied threat is powerful and management approaches which are sensitive to these internal fears contribute most to reductions in tension and in threats of dangerous behaviour. This always means a change of perspective and it requires substantial clinical teaching and professional supervision of care staff to introduce them to these new approaches and attitudes to their work. Careful working-through of these understandings is necessary to encourage care staff to think about disturbed behaviour and its meanings, before new management ideas can be accepted and put into practice.

To view the problems of violence and aggression in this way requires a distinct change of vertex. It is not easy, in the case of a violent, disruptive patient, for care staff to shift focus from the perception of him as a dangerous menace, to a view of him as driven by confusions and fears which fill *him* with persecution and panic.

In our institutions for the learning-disabled, as well as in other residences caring for disruptive and challenging clients, one of the most important concepts to introduce and the hardest for care staff to accept is the idea that the violent client who seems to be in charge, in a reign of terror, is very far from being in control. The greatest disruptions come from those who cannot control *themselves* and are themselves in fear of explosion, and this is what creates fear in others too. It is harder to understand that the perpetrator is also in fear and panic and that his panic requires containment, not extinction by the carer. The more the violent individual is treated as if he were in control and accountable for his actions, the more likely he is to be stimulated to further outbursts.

The violent patient's controlling of others by intimidation is not to be confused with strength, however much it may masquerade as such.

Paradoxically, the containment of such threatening behaviour is often achieved by less, not more effort to wrest control from the intimidator. Indirect interventions in which threatening behaviour is contained by environmental supports and controls is usually more successful because it does not put pressure on the already weak ego structure of the violent individual who feels his self-control to be in such jeopardy, in contrast to his presentation of apparent but spurious strength.

CONTAINMENT

Psychoanalytical observation certainly cannot afford to be confined to perception of what is verbalised only: what of more primitive uses of the tongue?

(Bion 1970)

As introduced by Bion, containment is a sophisticated concept which has now become central to modern psychoanalysis. Its application in the field of learning disability is less familiar but of such importance that it merits some detailed discussion.

To understand violent behaviour, it is necessary to return to its roots in infantile rage and panic and to the terrors of disintegration which threaten the emergent sense of self in the infant, when there is insufficient experience of containment. Bion's concept of containment derives from the mechanism of projective identification introduced by Klein. She describes one aspect of this mechanism as being concerned with the modification of infantile fears; the infant projects its unbearable feelings into a mother who receives and accommodates them for a time, making them tolerable and acceptable again to the child. In this sense, the mother can be considered to be providing a 'container' for the infant's unbearable feelings, and these Bion designates as the 'contained'.

Bion used this model of containment, the container into which an object can be projected, and the object that can be projected into it, which he termed the contained, as a representation of the interaction fundamental to mental growth. When container and contained are conjoined, they are suffused by emotion, and in this lies the vitality of the conjoined objects. Psychic development proceeds on this model which, optimally, promotes growth in both container and contained. Mental growth, in Bion's view, is not a slow gradual process, but timeless, more a series of catastrophic conjunctions which, if the operation of containment is working well, results in insight and learning but when working badly means either frustration and incomprehension or escape into omniscience. The conjunction of container and contained is dynamic and the more container and contained are disjoined and denuded of emotion (in the service of avoiding the frustrations of contact with the pain of growth and life) the more lifeless each becomes and the more they approximate the inanimate (Bion 1962b). Container and contained may relate through proximity but there is no enlivening spark.

To denote and represent the abstraction of his model of this container–contained relationship, Bion uses the female symbol as the abstraction representing the container and the male symbol for the contained. He uses these signs deliberately but they are not intended to be limited to their sexual connotations. The sexual association conveys the dynamic nature of containment in this sense, in contrast to the concept of containment as ring-fencing, with which it is not to be confused.

The relationship between container and contained may be commensal, symbiotic or parasitic. In the commensal relationship, contained and container are dependent on each other for mutual benefit without modifying or harming each other. This allows and fosters the mental growth of both, as in the mother–child example above. In the symbiotic relationship, one depends on the other to mutual advantage, but in a way which includes reciprocal modifications which is, limiting to further development. The parasitic relationship is destructive to both and destroys the possibility of growth.

The earliest relationship between mother and infant may be considered as a part-object relationship, that between mouth and breast. In terms of Bion's abstraction, that is between contained (hunger, the impulse to suckle) and container (breast), and it is this relationship which, according to Bion, becomes internalised by the infant as the basic model of the apparatus for dealing with thought. Pre-conceptions, or innate expectations, mate with sense-impressions which realise the pre-conceptions to produce conceptions. He illustrates with the model of the baby exploring an object by putting it in his mouth.

This model for the growth of learning means learning *from* experience. The capacity for taking in sense impressions develops along with the capacity for awareness of sense data. The container–contained conjunction is the model for Bion's concept of 'alpha function', the basic equipment for thinking, and for learning. It is essentially an emotional experience affording a sense of satisfaction when the relationship prospers. In the early feeding situation hunger is satiated but the experience of love in that situation is as essential to the infant's mental growth as the milk is to its physical survival. From simple beginnings in a limited number of biologically determined preconceptions associated with the survival of the organism (feeding, breathing and excretion), learning patterns grow increasingly more complex in the course of the growth of both container and contained. Alternatively, if the emotion which suffuses the conjunction of contained container is intense envy this may even be strong enough to destroy contact with the liveness of objects, including the self. In these circumstances, relationships survive only in dead, automaton-like ways.

The discovery of this somato-psychic foundation for mental development led Bion to emphasise that the investigation of the development and nature of thought and the apparatus used for dealing with thought was fundamental to the understanding of psychotic disorder. This means that in the investigation of mental illness the examination of thought and the factors involved in the development of thinking must take precedence over considerations of the content of thought contributing to the breakdown. This injunction is even more apposite in the case of the learning-impaired. Tustin counsels similarly when she emphasises the primitive, pre-verbal levels of disturbance involved in autism and childhood psychosis, where the child is immersed in a sensory, not a psychic world. The foundations of primitive thinking are laid down in association with the formation of paranoid-schizoid structures, and disruptions of the preliminary links which would allow conscious awareness of sense impressions at this level mean that the individual does not reach paranoid-schizoid constructions but is left isolated in an uncomprehending sensory world, as Tustin has so vividly portrayed.

Children with autism, of whom many are numbered among the learning-impaired, are not, therefore, in conflict with their objects, nor are they confused by distortions of perceptions of their objects. They cannot even be said to have withdrawn from the object. Instead, they have attached themselves desperately to sensations, lost, as one patient put it, 'in aeons of space', with only bodily sensations to hold on to, to protect from falling into the abyss. It is a highly perverse world where all the biologically given means of communication are turned to self-stimulation of the most primitive kind. Preoccupation with sensations takes the place of the feelings which might otherwise have developed to ensure the availability of mental elements and this means the blocking and immobilising of the development of mind. Such individuals are beset with terrors of uncontainment and dreads of spilling out or of falling for ever and of losing the sense of continuity of existence.

Tustin has most graphically described such experiences, not the same as a fear of death, which is conceptualised and has some shared meaningfulness. A depth of dread and terror which has to be so desperately defended against is, literally, unimaginable, and a measure of this is that in some personalities psychosis or suicide is the defence against it.

Descriptions of such experiences remain to a large extent speculative and depend on the clinical observations and interpretations of highly experienced and sensitive clinicians. However, these are now being steadily supplemented by the retrospective accounts of writers recalling their own early autistic or psychotic experiences. Temple Grandin (Grandin and Scariano 1986) in the United States and Donna Williams (1992) in Australia are two of the most recent and both confirm the predominance of incomprehension and fear in their earliest memories. Bemperad (1979) described the recollections of a young man who at the age of four had been diagnosed autistic by Kanner. Bemperad speaks of his surprise at hearing of the intensity of fear and terror that was remembered by this man, which seemed to contrast so directly with 'the unperturbed, and serene external appearance of autistic children'.

FRUSTRATION AND INCOMPREHENSION

The container–contained configuration also appears in the formation and limitations of words. The word is the product of the containment of sense data to form a constant conjunction, the word binding together the conjunction of these elements into entities which can be identified as meaningful. The same model applies to communication, which is about the relationship between meaning and its expression, optimised in the commensal relationship. A word contains meaning or alternatively a meaning can contain a word, if the appropriate word can be found. At times, feelings can be so powerful that the capacity for verbal expression of them breaks down, resulting in either incoherence and stuttering or paralysis and stony silence. Thus the constant conjunction may destroy the word but, conversely, the meaningfulness of the constant conjunction may be forced out by the word, when the word is already saturated by pre-existing associations. The development of language seems likely to have proceeded on the basis of such a balancing of pressures to contain meaning and feeling.

In the case of marked learning-impairment, the capacity to verbalise is often severely restricted with consequent absence of meaning and limitations in communication and comprehension. The patient can be at a loss to express meaning, or his meaning may be too intense to express properly. Such are the conditions for motor discharge, instead of thinking. Talking, shouting, aggressiveness or other muscular movement are the ways of discharging tension in an evacuatory procedure very different from the containing processes required for communication.

The ejective process which is employed to rid the psyche of unwanted elements, to avoid thinking and awareness of feeling, is pathological. It is a radical and ruthless dissociation from psychic content, not the same as the normal processes described by Freud (1911) in which, under the conditions of pleasure principle, action and motor discharge are associated with 'disencumbering the personality of accretions of stimuli'. Under these very different pathological conditions, a smile or a statement, for example, has to be interpreted as 'an evacuatory muscular movement and not as a communication of feeling' (Bion 1962b). Such a breakdown of the thinking equipment leads to a mental life dominated by inanimate objects and a patient who feels dead and who has great difficulty in experiencing that from which he might learn. Such thinking as is possible at this level may be adequate to deal with the inanimate and with what can be seen and dealt with concretely and this is why the mentally impaired are often attributed more understanding than they possess.

Bion's work on human thinking and its evolution has brought about some new advances in the field of learning impairment, where the benefits of a fresh approach have allowed new understandings of learning disorder to be opened up. His theory has a universal application, because it is concerned with the development of mental capacities. It does not necessarily follow that psychoanalysis is an appropriate form of treatment for all mental conditions, but it does mean that a new means of illuminating previously incomprehensible behaviour patterns has become available to us. Some of the obscurities and perplexities encountered in the behaviour of the learning-impaired have received clarification too from Tustin's differentiation of encapsulated and confusional states, two conditions frequently to be found among the learning-impaired. In a field where new thinking has been scarce, and hard to come by, these contributions bring relief and encouragement and renewed hope. These are creative ideas which put a new face on the nature of the behavioural disturbances which so often present major challenges to caretakers and, as such, the possibility of relief which they offer is worthy of attention.

MANAGEMENT CONCEPTS REVISED

The psychoanalytic understanding of mental development, because it stresses the emotional underpinnings essential to the growth of cognitive abilities, has important implications for the management of the learning-impaired. Policies which do not recognise the intrinsically dynamic basis of learning and which regard learning as a gradual process of training and habituation, tend to stress the setting of goals with various incentives for success. Programmes for normalisation, equally, disregard the inherent difficulties I have described in this chapter and in so doing raise expectations unrealistically.

When care staff are encouraged to embark on training programmes, with the intention of showing gradual improvements, a frequent outcome is the weakening of confidence and enthusiasm as results dwindle or even become counter-productive. Morale is weakened when staff become frustrated and disheartened by failure to produce the anticipated results and confidence in being able to achieve any improvement at all steadily drains away.

However disconcerting, it is important to note the degree of divergence that exists between traditional management policies based on learning theory and those that are informed by psychoanalysis. In many instances, the implications for policy or strategy in particular situations would mean that the recommended practices would be so different as to be diametrically opposed, as the examples below will illustrate. What is significant and different and offers to bring some encouragement is that the new and distinctive approach to 'challenging behaviour' and to learning-impairment reduces considerably the pressures on care staff to be able to demonstrate individual improvements in behaviour and achievement. Instead, the reduction of tension, disturbance and violence is achieved by the creation of an atmosphere of safety. Confidence comes from a supportive, meaningful and orderly environment which is neither indulgent nor punitive.

Potentially dangerous individuals experience severe threats to their own peace of mind and their disturbed behaviour usually conceals a high degree of sensitivity. The regime which fosters a sense of safety and security is therefore much more likely to induce temperateness and an atmosphere conducive to learning than one which, by emphasising the setting of goals and targets, is provocative of frustration. The safe, secure regime does not mean laissez-faire, still less does it imply a soft, compliant environment. The secure atmosphere is one in which there is firmness and consistency of management and a clear understanding of priorities which is shared by all staff. With this approach, the training, professionalism and discipline of the care staff is the first priority and takes precedence over ideas concerning the training and discipline of the clients.

Firmness, reliability and consistency in managing disturbed behaviour are born of understanding. It is not enough simply to be benevolent and empathic. Understanding is essential to the creation of the
predictable, containing environment which promotes security, and it is
this feeling of safety which is necessary to dispel the fears and anxieties
which lead to disturbance and violence. To introduce management
practices of this kind into the care of the learning-impaired does call for
substantial improvements in the training and professionalism of care
staff. However, with the latter already seriously under-trained, it would
be true to say that any policy which is designed to train, control or
facilitate the development of impaired individuals but which is
delivered by untrained and psychologically unsophisticated staff, is
likely to produce as many problems as it is designed to reduce.

For example, relatively simple concepts used to change behaviour,
like distraction or inducement, may be regarded as harmless or even
benign, but when unexpected results are produced, they can only be
interpreted as inexplicable. A brief episode in the management of one
learning-impaired seven-year-old illustrates the predicament for
psychoanalytically uninformed staff.

Terry was a boy who had exhibited severe confusional disturbance
since infancy and he was brought into residential care when his parents
finally found him too difficult to control. His one preoccupation was
with jigsaw puzzles. He was highly skilled and very speedy but he stuck
always to the same puzzle. Recognising aptitude and ability, his main
carer wanted to move him on, to encourage some development and
expansion of his capacities. The care worker was prepared for slow
progress and even a change of jigsaw would have been welcomed as an
advance. However, Terry could not be distracted from his attachment to
the familiar puzzle, and the carer finally decided to take this away and
hide it, so as to free Terry, he thought, to take an interest in the new one.
Terry reacted strongly at first and this was expected. It was when his
behaviour began to grow more and more disturbed in the next week or
two, and included indications that he was hallucinating, that it was
difficult for staff to believe that the loss of the jigsaw puzzle could have
been so important to him, particularly in the context of their intentions
to help the boy's development, not to punish him.

Terry's preoccupation with the jigsaw puzzle had to be understood
not simply in terms of his behaviour and interests but in terms of its
containing function in giving him a task which he could master and
complete. The jigsaw became a concrete experience of containment to
which he was deeply attached, in the absence of an internalised

experience of containment which could be generalised, enabling him to engage in other activities. Terry sought to fill his time with these activities to avoid feeling dissatisfaction or frustration. The experience of relief, in Terry's case, resulted not from feelings of satisfaction, but came from the very different experience of being able to rid himself of tension through his repeated activities. He had some language capacity, but it was inadequate to meet the requirements of emotional containment and the verbal expression of thoughts or feelings. Equally, his understanding of the words he used was unequal to the task of taking in and of comprehending the care worker's intentions.

Sound foundations for the articulation of verbal thought can be laid insofar as the assimilating and introjectory processes remain intact, and in Freud's words 'turned to the relations between object impressions' (Freud 1911), and are not exploded away by evacuative projection. When the projective evacuative processes predominate, verbal thought is compromised at the outset and instead of the linking, relating and articulating processes which produce learning, there is, in Bion's words, a heightened effort to force the fragmented elements of experience into indiscriminate, inappropriate 'agglomerations' (Bion 1957). Terry's 'skill' with jigsaw puzzles, a common accomplishment of children with autism, reflects this 'mindless' state. Like most autistic children, his interest in the puzzle is not led by comprehension of the task and the use of the pictorial cues, but is limited to the perception of shape, and the puzzle can as easily be completed upside-down as right way up.

In children like Terry, where development has been compromised before the achievement of language, with its emotionally containing function, the difficulties can best be recognised in the failure to achieve narrative. Words and phrases learnt from copying may be available, but the coherence of narrative necessary to communication is missing and gives a boring, deadening quality to personal contacts. Echolalic verbalisation, immediate or distant, has not achieved a connection with meaningfulness and a further source of confusion and frustration arises if such language is regarded as an indication of intellection, or if its emptiness is too readily compensated by meaning furnished by the listener!

CONCLUSIONS

The approach to learning impairment which I have been advocating in this chapter emphasises how much patience and care is required of those who work in the face of the huge impatience, indifference, negligence and recklessness to be found among the learning-impaired. The lack of emotional containment to which I have drawn attention constitutes, in my view, the primary deficiency, whatever the factors, emotional, constitutional or biological, contributory to that failure. This fundamental deficiency means that, for development to be set in motion, the necessary emotional containment requires to be found in abundance in the environment, that is in the organisation and structure of the social and educational environment and in the personal emotional capacities of the professional staff. The hopelessness and despair which have to be tolerated by care workers take the form of giving up and giving in, the twin adversaries to be resisted in the struggle to promote co-operation and interest.

I do not underestimate the difficulties involved in bringing about so radical a change of approach, when it demands something of an act of faith. Carers are resistant to adopting attitudes and techniques which seem to defy their own conscious reasoning and it would require serious preparatory work, in addition to on-going psychoanalytic supervision, for staff to be able to bring about significant changes of attitude and policy. Apart from a few scattered instances of psychoanalytic supervision by individual psychologists, there has as yet been little serious attempt to employ psychoanalytic ideas in the management and care of the learning-disabled in our National Health Service institutions. The theoretical and clinical advances in our understanding of the processes of mental development (Bion 1962a) have already brought beneficial changes to the practice of psychoanalysis and individual psychoanalytic psychotherapy and these advances in understanding now need to be turned to the advantage of those providing for the needs of the learning-impaired. Tustin's work in treating individual autistic children has helped to demonstrate the pre-verbal, sensory-dominated states which characterise the mental disability in autism. She has been able to present us with a picture of a world that is so different from our own experience that her findings require attention.

Every avenue of new understanding which might have an impact on this field needs to be investigated, not least because of the possibility of affording help to those who try to work amid the challenges and confusions of such learning disability. Besides, these challenges continue to increase, as more and more violent individuals are having to be contained in the community. Bion has made it clear in his writing, and it has been amply illustrated in the work of Tustin, that the understanding of pre-verbal states is the key to understanding human development and its disturbances. The illumination of the phenomena of learning-impairment is contingent, therefore, on the investigation of the pre-verbal components of communication, and psychoanalytic theory now provides the most appropriate tool for this.

Chapter 12

The restoration of god

And the light shineth in darkness; and the darkness comprehended it not.

St John 1:5

The environment into which Frances Tustin was born was filled with religious fervour and devotion. Her parents were both believers and followers of the Christian gospel and their lives were dedicated to the Church and its works. They were good people who believed passionately in the salvation of souls but, as their daughter has wryly remarked, concern for their immortal souls tended to outweigh regard for their lives or hers, on this earth. Both belonged to the Church of England, but came, so to speak, from different ends of that institutional spectrum, her mother's High Church traditions contrasting vividly with her father's non-conformist history. Their conflicts and arguments were always about religious matters as each tried to establish their respective understanding of truth. Communion with God as the fountain of goodness and truth was of vital importance to two people so serious-minded and sincere in their desire to live a good life, but religious beliefs divided them instead of bringing them together. Relationships with their deity were, at best, symbiotic and did not leave room for the emotional reality of their relationship with one another. Paradoxically, this prevented them from living the lives they desired and separated them from the very ideals which they each preached.

Their difficulties ran deep and were more than the sum of personality conflicts and differences of tradition or religious dogma. They were engaged in a deep search to understand themselves and their place in the world but their thoughts dismissed the emotional reality and meaningfulness of their lives together as inferior and, instead, turned away from their humanity to their divinity; towards religious ideals which then became a sterile battleground. Sister Minnie saw the animal passions of human beings as frightening and sinful, something from which to be saved rather than to prosper. She strove tirelessly to live the life of a good woman but, with a mind devoted to the divine, her grasp of ordinary life was slight and she saw no virtue in intellectual enquiry.

Human curiosity and epistemophilia, constantly pushing at the frontiers of darkness, present a continuing challenge to psychic containment in the pressures to accommodate new ideas and to allow the growth of thinking. The frustrations and fears inherent in the processes of learning have their roots in the heritage of primitive animal impulse with its deep, instinctive antagonism to the delays necessary for thinking. Religious man avoids these conflicts and responsibilities by seeking to be at one with a deity in whom ultimate truth resides. In the Vickers household, this was Mother's path to enlightenment. She did not countenance any new thought, believing that she had found the truth, and she regarded the intellectual curiosity and psychological explorations of her day as a sin. For Father, the freedom to think was too much to contain and he embraced the philosophy of anarchism which allowed responsibility for containing thinking to be exploded under the guise of spontaneity and liberty. He was ambivalent about the truth which he thought he had found and, in the end, he returned to the path of his wife. Their daughter turned her investigatory gifts to thinking about the thinking processes and to exploring the rudiments of a sensory containment in those who, unable to imagine life at all, exist in the external world, but live in deepest mental darkness.

THE LIGHT OF MYTHOLOGY

Bion considered the human capacity for thought still to be at an embryonic stage of its development and his work has concentrated on the search to identify patterns and configurations in human thinking which remain constant over time and over widely differing contexts. From such patterns he sought to isolate the invariants which might help to throw some light on the way our minds work. The history of myth and religion provided a field abundant in relics of early attempts by human beings to use their minds to understand the world they lived in and their place in it.

In mythology, Bion found a rich source of evidence for the consistency of certain configurations and he regarded the myth as a valuable fact-finding tool which he used in his investigation of thinking. Myths are stories about origins, accounts of how things began. They tell a story about how something came into being. They are expressions of ideas about natural forces or phenomena and, although expressed in primitive, pictorial form, have importance as the primitive counterpart to sophisticated scientific formulation. Whilst scientific observation attempts to introduce more precision, it is less well equipped to register the emotional vitality conveyed in the myth which has its own significance. The importance of this is particularly prominent in the case of psychoanalytic observation, where the objects of study are not sensuous but psychic.

At the beginning of this century, the striking similarities between the contents of myths and the world of the unconscious were pointed out by both Freud (1913) and Jung (1919). In Freud's work, the role of myth in furthering his investigations and its contribution to the discovery of psychoanalysis have brought universal acknowledgement to the Oedipus story (Freud 1900). Myths have an existential function, dealing with the basic themes of human survival, themes which are common to different mythologies throughout the world. Myths about the creation of humankind, for instance, appear to be universal, and stories of cosmic cataclysm are also widespread.

To Freud's oedipal theory, Bion adds his observations of further facets of the story which illuminate functions of the personality other than the sexual elements (Bion 1963). He sees Oedipus as 'the triumph of determined curiosity over intimidation' and, as such, a symbol of scientific investigation. Since the constant theme is curiosity in the personality about the personality, the links with psychoanalytic investigation are conspicuous. This aspect of the oedipal myth gains conviction when brought into conjunction with the themes of other myths and the resulting configuration assumes particular relevance when applied to the primitive stages of the development of the apparatus of learning.

Disengaging from the separate narratives of the stories, Bion selects those elements in each which he regards as repeated references to a common theme, the sin of curiosity. He considers the warnings of Tiresias and considers this aspect of the oedipal myth in conjunction with the myth of Eden, and the attack on speech in the infliction of confusion of tongues in the Babel myth. All of these display different facets of hostility towards knowledge and the punishment and banishment which will be the consequence of attempts to acquire it. He detects a similar pattern in the disasters of the self-inflicted punishments of the Sphinx and Oedipus. The underlying configuration which he brings into focus from these scattered references contained in the stories is the specific warning of the dire consequences which follow curiosity and the pursuit of learning. The message of Christ much later was couched in more benign terms but also seems to counsel against thinking – 'I am the way, the truth, and the life: no man cometh unto the Father, but by me' (St John 14:6).

Bion does not displace existing theory, but expands its application to deeper levels of functioning when the oedipal theme is treated as a private myth relating to the individual's primitive stages of developing an apparatus for learning. The mythical stories of creation and destruction he found relevant to his hypothesis of the attacks on the earliest form of thinking which result in psychotic disorder. His formulations concentrate on the need to uncover those primitive psychic factors which continue to present a major threat to the advances of self-knowledge and to the future development of thinking. The problem appears to be one in which humans become persecuted by the very mental development they seek to achieve.

Klein has described disturbed patients in whom the violence of the attack on the object results not only in the disintegration of the object but of the self, too (Klein 1946). Bion (1962a) extended Klein's theory of projective identification to propose a pathological form of splitting characterised by fragmentation which is catastrophic to normal mental development. When reality cannot be tolerated, the apparatus which enables awareness of it is destroyed. Dire consequences again, and such are the conditions of psychosis when destruction of the capacity to think results in exile from reality and human emotional contact. This is where there is an intersection with the scenarios of explosive rage, punishment and banishment which are embedded in the imagery of mythology. The evolution of the human psyche and the transition from animal instinct and impulse to human consciousness and the capacity for mentation have proceeded, it would seem, on a basis of continuing conflict between the forces of containment and those of disintegration with an ever-present threat of catastrophic breakdown.

Bion sees the human evolutionary struggle to communicate and to be at one with the truth as a model for the personality. The understanding of disturbances to thinking, together with the possibility of the further evolution of human thinking, have, therefore, a common basis in the task of reconciling a primitive animal nature with a capacity to contain and transform its outbursts in verbal communication. His formulation of a theory of the origins of thinking proposes the existence of a pre-cursory level of mental, or rather what he termed 'proto-mental', activity, different from but an essential basis for later forms. This concerns the struggle to know psychic qualities and depends on the outcome of the emotional events which occur between a mother and her infant and which are decisive to the establishment – or not – of a capacity to think in the infant. The corollary of this theory is the interesting and original idea that knowledge of the psychological precedes and facilitates knowledge of the physical world, and this insight carries significant implications for the further development of thinking and of society.

THE COMING OF THE IMMORTALS

Every people in the world has its own myths, and the modern scientific study of mythology (Frazer 1922) has established that there are many similarities in the stories of peoples of widely different culture and race, living far apart in time and geographical space. The evidence of myth suggests that humans, in meeting the challenges to their physical and mental survival, have reacted in much the same way the world over. Myths are attempts to make sense of a world which to primitive humans would have been unpredictable and alarming, not unlike, perhaps, the terrifying and unpredictable world of the autistic child which Tustin has tried to evoke. The early myth is an attempt to explain the world as it is experienced but does little to introduce the order and predictability needed to provide the essentials for containment of fear and to begin the process of moderation of primitive terror. This was introduced by the coming of the immortals in Greek mythology.

The immortals were thought to people all the hills and valleys, woods and streams of the lands of Greece and even the sea around them. The early Greeks pictured the immortals as very much like themselves but much more powerful and beautiful and free. Ideal people, but also free of the 'coils' of mortality, and this important distinction also meant the identification of time as a factor in human existence. The presence of the immortals introduced a sense of stability in the continuity of their existence and it was not long before they came to be referred to as the gods, as they are in the stories of Homer. Homeric gods were not significantly differentiated from humans and when Homer was criticised by later Greek philosophers for his anthropomorphism, this saw the beginning of the attempt to free the concept of divinity and of ideals from self-centred human preoccupations. It instituted these ideal and omnipotent qualities outside humans, separating them from the gods, and this splitting marked a significant step in the development of thinking. It was essential to mental growth for humans to be able to distinguish between themselves as ordinary human beings and the view of themselves as omnipotent and omniscient, and this was facilitated by differentiating the gods and endowing them with these qualities.

The creation of the gods demonstrated a degree of self-recognition, particularly in the naming and identification of feelings, motives, and human activities which were represented by individual gods. Their separation and idealisation belonged to the stage of paranoid-schizoid organisation and constituted a necessary step in differentiation. A degree of order and to some extent safety would have been achieved by reducing confusion and unpredictability, a function which, down the centuries, religions have continued to fulfil. As I understand him, Bion draws a parallel between the public history of myth and religion and the private history of individual mental development. The separation of god and human was a useful cultural development but it was made possible only after human relationships could achieve sufficient self-containment to identify feelings and to distinguish between subject and object. With the concept of twoness, another 'people' could be imagined:

What forms are these coming
so white through the gloom?
What garments out-glistening
The gold-flowered broom?

First hymn they the Father
of all things; and then
The rest of immortals,
The action of men.

Matthew Arnold, 'Empedocles on Etna' (1852)

In the first stage of idealisation, the immortals and the gods were barely distinguished from human beings. The second stage involved the establishment of the separation between god and human being which differentiated between the finite human and the infinite and transcendent god. In the third stage religion is concerned with awareness of the good qualities of which humans have been deprived by the projections into the deity, and reunion with these 'divine' attributes becomes the dominant theme. The separation of god and human in this way has a parallel in the separation of thinking and feeling which is inherent in disturbed development of the personality and characterises thought disorder. Following these divides, the undertow, in both spheres, despite formidable resistance, is towards reunion and integration.

DARKNESS AND EXILE IN THE WORLD OF AUTISM

The advent of the gods represented a point of advance in human thinking and depended on the development of a capacity for imagination.

Magical omnipotent thinking as the forerunner of reality testing is a necessary stage in mental development. Those who cannot see the immortals, remain in darkness. A sense of human identity, individual and group, was a necessary correlate to this imaginative leap of envisaging beings different from humans. The moment of critical developmental significance is perhaps best expressed in the story of the coming together of body and soul in the union of Cupid and Psyche.

People with autism are characterised by their aloofness and indifference to live meaningful contact with other human beings (Wing and Gould 1979) or indeed with their own bodies, often treated as if inanimate. In conjunction with this, they display an absence of empathy and a lack of imagination which has been experimentally demonstrated (Baron-Cohen *et al.* 1985). According to psychoanalytic theory, internalisation of their experience of the world is minimal and they are dominated by projection as a means of finding relief from overwhelming anxiety. Not for them the formation of any 'forms in the gloom' but instead, as Tustin has so vividly portrayed, a desperate terror of blackness and emptiness and exile from meaning. Whether the autistic individual is a Kanner type, frozen and, in Tustin's terms, emotionally encapsulated, or is emotionally and perceptually confused, in Tustin's terms entangled, it would not be inappropriate to describe him as a godless creature.

Serious disturbances of the balance of projection and introjection which inhibit or destroy capacities for internalisation and the growth of a sense of self preclude also the possibility of idealisation (and the conception of a deity) and demonstrate the far-reaching significance of factors belonging in the earliest experiences of life. The infant's relationship with a mother is the prototype for getting to know the world and the self and the place of the self in the world. The autistic child is different and limited in his capacity to 'know' anything or to use his mind for thinking about his world in the sense which Bion used in his theory of thinking. Bion introduced the symbol K to designate the emotional experience involved in the fundamental form of thinking necessary to comprehending reality and gaining insight and understanding of oneself and others. K indicates a relationship with the object in thinking, as there is in love (L) and hate (H). If xKy, then 'x is in the state of getting to know y and y is in a state of getting to be known by x'. What is strikingly different about the autistic child is the absence of K.

The autistic child relies predominantly on his eyes to explore the world and, while this can be developed to a very high degree of acuity and sensitivity, it is, by itself, a perceptual mode unfitted to the emotional task of getting to know people. Avoidance of eye-contact with others, which is also a characteristic, is not to be confused with loss of interest, for the visual sensitivity and sharpness of the autistic child can be satisfied by the most fleeting of glances. It is when hearing and listening are combined with looking that the most lively chords are struck between human beings and this can be observed at its most energetic in the delighted physical responsiveness which accompanies the early cooing responses in babies as they watch and listen to a lovingly attentive mother.

The autistic child uses other perceptual modalities in addition to looking, particularly the tactile and olfactory, but, notably, does not readily conjoin looking with listening. Listening is the means of getting to know about how other people think and feel and means taking something in, aurally and psychologically. When the balance of the primitive introjective-projective processes is heavily weighted on the side of projection and evacuation of anxiety rather than the taking in of meaningfulness and reassurance, the eyes are the principal vehicles of that projection. Eyes are poetically referred to as the windows of the soul and windows allow the passage of light in both directions, inwards and outwards. To rely on looking and on visual cues creates maximum opportunity for confusions and reversals between inside and outside while the closing off of auditory cues drastically reduces the ingress of perceptual stimuli.

Clinicians of all theoretical persuasions confirm these characteristics (Meltzer *et al.* 1975, Wing 1981, Frith 1989, Alvarez 1992, among others). Reid (1990) describes a gradual reuniting of looking and listening in a traumatised two-year-old which heralded the unfreezing of autistic defences and the incipient growth of an appreciation of the therapist as a source of life and understanding.

The emotional deadness of autism seems closely related to the disjunction of looking and listening, the two principal receptive modes which, coming together, produce the 'big bang' of recognition and response. Murray has recorded striking evidence on film of the qualitative differences in infant behaviour when optimal conjunction is compromised or disturbed (Murray and Trevarthen 1985, Murray 1992). I shall not here take up the mother–infant components in the development of the capacity to internalise experience for my focus is on the examination of those states of psychic isolation and darkness which exist in autism and which Tustin has tried to illuminate. When 'hypertrophy' of projective processes floods the apparatus for developing mentation, because of overwhelming panic and fear, it would seem that the individual is exiled in an external world of concrete objects, including people, which he can quite literally see, but cannot comprehend because of minimal operation of introjective processes.

Henceforth, such development as it is possible to continue will be at the level of an automaton, where watching and copying the object confers a semblance of human living but leaves the individual isolated and lonely, as in the cases of Sam and Sarah, discussed in Chapter 10. Frith perceives the same disjuncture when she discusses an extract from the autobiography of an autistic young man who complains, just like Sam, that he is lonely and wants a companion but does not understand the nature of human relationship or how he comes to be so much on the outside of life: 'Perhaps someone reading this will get in touch with me. I hope someone that can offer me some love and affection will get in touch' (David's Autobiography, quoted in Frith 1989). The loneliness and the emptiness are touching, but the passivity of the appeal is incongruous.

In the extremes of autism, even the simulation of life holds no attraction and many autistic persons would be content, if undisturbed, to remain withdrawn in their sensory fortresses with brief forays into human contact only when the demands of survival required it. A less uncompromising withdrawal is found in obsessional pathology where the world of external objects can sometimes be turned to some good account but where the world of relationships remains inscrutable and elusive. Extreme cases of obsessional pathology offer another entry to the world of psychotic fear and panic because those experiences can be confirmed by obsessionals which to a large extent remain inaccessible in the autistic. The obsessional acts upon his experiences in the external world and the following picture gives a glimpse of the magnitude of the problem when terrors of uncontainment and the psychotic dread of running out or dissolving away are dominant.

MAX

Max came for assessment because it was becoming more and more difficult for medical and social agencies to find an appropriate placement for him. His importunate searching for 'help' was exhausting all the professionals with whom he came into contact and my experience in the assessment interview provided ample confirmation. There was a flow of words which hardly stopped. Some of this conveyed a coherent story, some was highly confused and the whole was interspersed with complaints about and advice to the professionals whose help he thought he should have. At no time did there seem to be an indication of his expecting me to have anything to say and, indeed, he left little opportunity for me to speak.

I thought he was searching for an experience of containment of anxiety which threatened constantly to overwhelm him. All he seemed able to do was to discharge it and so he was forced to keep on doing so. His account of his desperate life described great concern about finding a containing object but his activities related to solutions in the external world and his emotional needs remained completely unrecognised.

Two concrete ways of trying to achieve containment were interesting although piteous. One was to search TV programmes for people he could feel some kinship with and he identified with those in whom he saw superior qualities of education, talent or breeding. His whole life was spent in making video recordings of chosen individuals and he collected so many tapes that his room was filled to capacity. Eventually he took to sleeping on the floor because his bed was also used to store tapes. The other idea he had was to write his thoughts down as a way of trying to understand something about his life, but again he was defeated and frustrated because he found that the pens ran out. As he complained to me about this, it seemed as if he felt there should exist a pen that would not run out but was capable of writing down for ever his unending anxiety. The running out of the pens was a recurring theme in this confused interview. Max was an unusually disturbed man whose early infant care was known to have been chaotic. He was now caught up in a compulsion to find a container which would provide him with a sense of boundary and continuity of existence but he was searching concretely in the external world for something which was essentially internal and emotional, which had been missing from his early infant experience and which he now could not recognise. He could only fill others with the incomprehension which overwhelmed him. He was in darkness about what it was he needed and he could not comprehend how it was that he could not find relief. I too was unable to find a way of helping him to see what I had to offer.

SALVATION

Autistic children, patients like Max and others whom I have described in this book, seem lost to the world of ordinary human contact and this is made all the more desolate by their desperate attachment to the external manifestations of life. Their plight is hard to imagine and it has been a major contribution of Tustin's work to help to conceptualise and illuminate such states which are pre-verbal and to do with the problem of experience which is unimaginable. How to retrieve from exile those who can barely believe in their own existence is a task that remains.

Tustin has described the children she has been able to help but she also recognises that the extent of the problems far outweighs the available resources and the capacities to understand and to help. Few patients in such dire states can be offered psychoanalytic help, but the work with those who have been has had great value in delineating the nature of the problem and contributes to improvements in the appropriateness of the provisions that can be made.

The *raison d'être* of embarking at all on the unequal struggle to 'reclaim' the lost souls lies in the opportunity to study the most primitive mental conditions when things go wrong and to discover there the factors necessary to the development of healthy minds. Alvarez has noted an important maternal function in what she has termed 'reclamation' which she came to discover in her long treatment of Robbie. This re-emphasises Tustin's claim that children with autistic pathology need to be treated as early in their lives as possible, before the powerful strategies of withdrawal become rigidified. This view is confirmed by Reid (1990) in a paper which notes a very speedy response to treatment in a severely withdrawn two-year-old.

The reclamation function of the therapist is important to recognise and reminds us of the container–contained dynamic where growth lies in the outcome of a *relationship* between the two. The maternal function of containment does not lie in being available as a passive receptacle in the way that Max treated me. The astonishing corollary to this attitude to containment was described to me by another obsessional patient, a young female graduate for whom the transition to a more dynamic sense of containment was slow and painful. Despite her intellectual achievements, she could not, she said, understand the processes of growth. She could only understand processes of accumulation or collection (cf. Bion's 'agglomeration') and although she could accept the evidence of growth, the process made no sense to her and was a continuing puzzle.

Reclamation and containment are functions of religion too and its historical development has been part of mental development and of our attempt to understand ourselves and our world. Religions continue to provide containment of anxiety for many by providing a structure that can be used as an alternative to emotional containment. Groups which emphasise salvation hold great comfort for those threatened by the 'black hole' of psychotic depression and for those torn by autistic and obsessional anxiety about their very existence. The experience of being 're-born' seems to relate to the finding of a new identity as a result of experiencing a new sense of containment in the deity. Religious containment often successfully replaces drugs and alcohol as a defence against

the terrors of disintegration and in this further demonstrates the significance of the concept of the container and the importance of finding
benign alternatives when internal resources are inadequate.

Religion seemed also to be the final resort of Tustin's patient Peter,
whose later obsessional defences were sufficient to allow some intellectual development but inappropriate to making meaningful personal,
emotional relationships. The mechanical quality of his life was finally
matched by an environment that could contain it and he found a place in
a Jewish religious sect where his life and his personal relationships were
given order and meaning in accordance with rules and rituals derived
from God. The containing and reclaiming function of religion remains
important to society but in the development of the integration of the
human mind what is to be sought, in Bion's words, 'is an activity that is
both the restoration of god (the mother) and the evolution of god (the
formless, infinite, ineffable, non-existent)'. From the influences of her
own religious background, Tustin's thinking has evolved in the course
of her researches in autism to bring a new depth of meaning to the
pressures and anxieties which troubled her parents. Her mother worked
for the souls of her Christian flock. Tustin has interested herself in those
whose grasp of the animate (Latin *animus*, the soul) is weak. She has
also brought to psychoanalysis the imaginative pictorial method of
thinking more characteristic of the myth which Bion wanted to restore
to research respectability. In her own distinctive and personal style, she
has provided us with an illuminating exposition of Bion's scientifically
sophisticated formulations which, for many, makes them more
accessible.

Glossary

Adhesive identification

A term first used by Esther Bick to describe a paper-thin relationship lacking emotional depth. Such relationships are easily and precipitately formed and frequently characterise the social lives of deprived children. Physical contact becomes a substitute for emotional life and anxiety is managed by frequently changing relationships. The concept of adhesive identification was elaborated by Meltzer who described such relationships as two-dimensional to emphasise the reduced capacity for mental containment.

Alpha function

An abstract term chosen by Bion to describe the most rudimentary form of thinking. The term is deliberately undefined so as not to encourage premature conceptualising of processes which are unknown. Alpha function operates on the sense impressions and on the emotions to produce alpha elements which are capable of being stored as memories and are suited to dream thought and conscious thought. They are primitive, ideographic and pre-verbal and the pre-requisites of symbolisation. If the patient cannot transform his emotional experience into alpha elements, he cannot dream. Freud pointed out the importance of the dream as the preserver of sleep so that when alpha function fails, the patient cannot dream and so cannot sleep. Clinically the psychotic state is one in which the patient is neither asleep nor awake.

Autistic object

These are usually hard objects used by autistic children to hold, arrange in order or to spin. They are used only for the child's specific purpose and are not played with in the normally appropriate way.

Autistic shapes

Sensations may be regarded as the forerunners of psychic life and Tustin introduced the term sensation 'shape' or sensation 'object' to describe the early sensory impressions. Compulsive or addictive preoccupations at this level which interfere with the development of socialising uses of sensation mean that sensation shapes become autistic sensation shapes or autistic shapes. The world of sensation which might have led to psychic development is thus, according to Tustin, used to block psychic growth.

Beta element

Beta elements are stored, but not in memories so much as in undigested facts. Bion regards beta elements as close to the Kantian idea of 'things in themselves' as distinct from phenomena. Beta elements are objects which can only be dealt with by evacuation in an effort 'to rid the psyche of accretions of stimuli' (Freud 1911) and are suited, therefore, to projective identification and to acting out.

Borderline

The term has a long history, referring traditionally to the border between neurosis and psychosis. It can be used to apply to neurotic patients not overtly displaying psychotic symptoms but who are seen clinically to be dealing with psychotic-level anxieties for which they have to make use of the mechanisms characteristic of psychosis.

Modern psychoanalysts have developed the concept further to give the name borderline to a particular mental structure in which the patient feels himself to be living on a border between inside and outside, between madness and sanity. This experience is also understood as indicating a level of development on the border between the paranoid-schizoid and the depressive positions formulated by Klein.

Conception/pre-conception

Terms used in Bion's theory of thinking to describe the biological precursors of the thinking processes. A pre-conception is an innate expectation like the infant's expectation that there is a nipple to go in the mouth. The pre-conception is realised by the experience of fulfilment of the expectation and this produces a conception. An established conception which can be named becomes a concept.

Death instinct

The concept of a death instinct was introduced by Freud in *Beyond the Pleasure Principle* (1920). It was his view that all organic instincts were essentially conservative. He saw them as directed towards the restoration of a former state rather than thrusting towards progress and change. From this point of view the advance of organic life has been a by-product of the striving to return to an initial state. Freud supported his contention with the argument that inanimate things existed before living creatures and that everything living dies and returns to the inanimate.

The death instinct continues to occupy an essential place in Kleinian theory but it remains controversial in psychoanalysis as a whole. It is a concept with a significance which has still to be fully understood.

Depressive position

This is a Kleinian concept indicating the new position reached by an infant (or an adult patient in analysis) when he realises that his love and his hate are directed towards the same person, the mother. The depressive position is closely associated with the experience of ambivalence and the capacity to tolerate ambivalence. There is concern for the object, felt to be damaged by the infant's hatred, and this is accompanied by reparative wishes. The term 'depressive' is somewhat misleading. Clinical depression is associated with failure to reach the depressive position and with fixation at the earlier paranoid-schizoid level and the pathological exaggeration of guilt.

Introjection

Introjection is the opposite of projection and refers to the process of internalising or taking in the experience of being cared for by an external object. The formation of internal representations of external objects and experience means the beginning of the mental structure of an internal world. Introjection is modelled on incorporation and is closely allied to identification. The development of the infant's relationship with his primary caregiver proceeds on the basis of balanced introjection and projection; projecting pain and anxiety into the object and taking in soothing care, security and love.

Narcissistic

Referring to the myth of Narcissus, Freud coined the term narcissism to denote a relationship-choice based on identification and self-reference.

Love is invested in an object chosen for its similarity to the self and represents a relationship with the self rather than with a clearly differentiated other. Affection, flattery, and idealisation are constantly required as supplies to counteract the emptiness of the narcissistic personality.

Object

The object as opposed to the subject was originally that which was needed to fulfil the desire or the instinctual need of the subject. In psychoanalysis, objects refer to persons or parts of persons or their symbols. Internal objects are derived from the experience of the relationship with the external objects and exist in psychic reality. The internal objects may or may not be congruent with the external objects. Objects may be experienced as good or bad, internal or external, whole or part. The maturity of the individual is contingent on a capacity to discriminate between internal and external, that is, between phantasy and reality.

Object relations theory

In psychoanalysis, object relations theory succeeded instinct theory as the central human concern came to be associated more with personal needs to relate to other persons and moved away from the Freudian idea of the reduction of instinctual tension. The concept of object relationship is now widely used in psychoanalysis in its broadest sense, to denote the individual's characteristic mode of relating to the world.

Obsessional

Obsessional features range from mild character traits of conscientiousness, orderliness, rationality and control of emotions to compulsive behaviours which the patient feels driven to repeat. In every case, the underlying threat is of anxiety and loss of control. In extreme cases, terror of loss of existence is experienced and threatens to be overwhelming. Confusion between internal and external means that action is taken in relation to the external world to control fears that belong in the internal phantasy world. Such actions are frequently repetitive or ritualistic.

Omnipotence

Phantasies of omnipotence refer to states of mind in which there is little distinction between internal and external. As a result, there is a belief that thoughts can influence the external world. Omnipotence is considered to be a characteristic of infantile thought which is moderated by experience and the growing capacity to tolerate the frustrations of reality. Omnipotent thinking is found in psychotic states and also underlies the thinking in primitive religion, ritual and magic.

Paranoid-schizoid position

The term introduced by Melanie Klein to indicate the infant's earliest attempt to structure his world. Aggressive instincts and libidinal wishes exist side by side from the beginning and splitting of the two indicates an attempt to master destructiveness. The infant splits his entire experience into good and bad parts and this includes his ego and his object representations. Bad experience is projected into a bad object which is then felt to be persecutory. The paranoid-schizoid position precedes the depressive position, but Klein's choice of the term position emphasises fluidity and on-going fluctuation between the paranoid-schizoid and depressive states. The paranoid-schizoid experience is of an 'all-or-nothing' world where anxiety is persecutory. It is a world of morality where there is little room for tolerance or doubt. Maturity increases with the admittance of emotional qualities of concern, tolerance of doubt, and a sense of guilt which characterise the depressive position. Paranoid-schizoid structures are dominant in the first four months of life, until depressive concern begins to be a moderating influence. Fluctuations between these two structurings of the mind, between two positions or vertices from which to view experience of the world, continue throughout life.

Projection

A term widely used and often in poorly defined ways. Its original geometric meaning refers to the correspondence of points on a figure between planes. It is used in this way in neurology, referring to the correspondence between peripheral receptor and central stimulation, the one being a projection of the other. Projection in psychology denotes that the subject perceives his or her environment in accordance with their own mental attributes, personality characteristics and interests. Freud referred to projection as a normal mechanism and Klein introduced projection as a part of the normal developmental process. Projection, a process modelled on the excretory functions, always concerns the expelling of that which cannot be recognised or tolerated in the self and its location in other people or things. However, the mechanism can also serve as a primitive means of communication. The baby, for example, projects feelings of distress, hunger or pain into the mother who gives them meaning and responds appropriately.

Projective identification

This expression was introduced by Melanie Klein to refer to the phantasied projection of split-off parts of the self (or the self as a whole) which are relocated in the object with which they are identified. Projective identification, as one mode of projection, is closely associated with the paranoid-schizoid mechanisms. The projection of the self or parts of the self into the object has the aim of control or possession of the object but it also results in depletion and impoverishment of the personality resources of the subject.

Splitting

A term employed by Freud to indicate the co-existence within the mind of two psychical attitudes to reality. The one takes account of reality while the other relies on denial and sees reality in terms of wishes and desire. It is this ego split which accounts for psychotic phenomena. Splitting of experience means that two incompatible attitudes to reality exist separately, side by side, without contact and without influencing one another and only one is experienced as the 'self'. The splitting of the ego and objects into two is associated with the paranoid-schizoid position. Bion has extended the concept of splitting to encompass a pathological form of splitting associated with disintegration and fragmentation of the ego. In this case experience is sliced into slivers rather than being divided into relatively integrated good and bad parts.

Transference

Transference phenomena were discovered clinically by Freud. They relate to the emergence of prototype infantile relationships in the context of specific adult relationships. Transference is not confined to psychoanalytic encounters but the relationship which facilitates the observation of transference phenomena par excellence is the analytic situation. Interpretations of 'the transference' are central to psychoanalytic treatment which is conducted within the arena of this relationship to the analyst where access is to be gained to all the basic problems presented in an analysis.

Chronology

1913	Born October 15th in Darlington where her parents were working in the Church of England.
1914	Father called to serve in First World War as Chaplain.
1919	Starts first school in Sheffield.
1923	Father becomes headmaster of a country village school and Frances is one of his pupils.
1924	Scholarship to Sleaford Girls' High School where she is a boarder.
1925	Father moves to another country school and Frances transfers to Grantham Girls' High School and becomes a day girl again.
1926	Irretrievable breakdown of the family when parents separate and Frances loses touch with her father.
1927	Mother returns to Sheffield to work as a Church Sister and Frances returns to school.
1930	Gains Higher School Certificate.
1931	Spends one year as a student teacher to help pay the forthcoming college fees.
1932	Enters Whitelands College, Putney, London, to train as a teacher.
1934	Qualifies as a teacher and returns to work in Sheffield in order to support her old and ailing mother.
1938	First marriage in Sheffield.
1940	Husband conscripted to serve in Second World War and posted abroad.
1941	Fortuitous opportunity to restore contact with father.
1942	Mother dies in Sheffield.
1943	Frances leaves Sheffield and joins a progressive educational community in Kent from where she can travel up to London in the evenings to attend the Child Development Course at London University.

1945   The end of the Second World War and the return of her husband to Sheffield.

1946   First marriage ends in divorce and Frances returns to Whitelands as a lecturer.

1948   Second marriage, to Arnold Tustin. Moves to Birmingham when Arnold becomes Professor of Electrical Engineering at Birmingham University.

1950   Commences the Child Psychotherapy Training at the Tavistock Clinic (commuting from Birmingham).

1951   Publication of her first book, *A Group of Juniors: A Study of Latency Children's Play.*

1953   Qualifies as a Child Psychotherapist.

1954   Honorary appointment at James Jackson Putnam Research and Treatment Center whilst spending a year in Massachusetts during Arnold's year as visiting Webster Professor at MIT.

1955   Arnold Tustin appointed Professor of Electrical Engineering at Imperial College, London, and they move their home to London.
Child Psychotherapist at Great Ormond Street Hospital.

1964   Moves home to Buckinghamshire and takes up a full-time post in Aylesbury Child Guidance Clinic on Arnold's retirement.

1971–3 Child Psychotherapist at the Tavistock Child Guidance Training Centre.

1972   Publication of *Autism and Childhood Psychosis.*

1973   Returns to Aylesbury Child Guidance Clinic full time.

1978   Retires from NHS work but continues to supervise and teach in this country and abroad.

1981   Publication of *Autistic States in Children.*

1984   Appointed Honorary Affiliate of the British Psychoanalytical Society.

1986   Publication of *Autistic Barriers in Neurotic Patients.*
Receives Honorary Membership of the Association of Child Psychotherapists.

1990   Publication of *The Protective Shell in Children and Adults.*

1993   Appointed Corresponding Member of the Psychoanalytic Center of California.

Publications by Frances Tustin

PAPERS

1958   'Anorexia Nervosa in an adolescent girl'. *British Journal of Medical Psychology*, 31 (3–4): 184–200.

1963   'Two drawings occurring in the analysis of a latency child'. *Journal of Child Psychotherapy*, 1 (1): 41–6.

1967   'Individual therapy in the clinic'. 23rd Child Guidance Inter-clinic Conference (NAMH, London).

1967   'Psychotherapy with autistic children'. *Bulletin of the Association of Child Psychotherapists*, 2 (3). Private circulation.

1969   'Autistic processes'. *Journal of Child Psychotherapy*, 2 (3): 23–39.

1973   'Therapeutic communication between psychotherapist and psychotic child'. *International Journal of Child Psychotherapy*, 2 (4): 440–50.

1978   'Psychotic elements in the neurotic disorders of children'. *Journal of Child Psychotherapy*, 4 (4): 5–18.

1980   'Psychological birth and psychological catastrophe'. In J. Grotstein (ed.) *Do I Dare Disturb the Universe?* London: Karnac.

1980   'Autistic objects'. *International Review of Psycho-Analysis*, 7 (1): 27–39.

1981   'A modern Pilgrim's Progress: reminiscences of analysis with Dr Bion'. *Journal of Child Psychotherapy*, 7: 175–9.

1981b   '"I"-ness: the emergence of the self'. *Winnicott Studies*, 1.

1983   'Thoughts on autism with special reference to a paper by Melanie Klein'. *Journal of Child Psychotherapy*, 9 (2): 119–31.

1984a   'Autistic shapes'. *International Review of Psycho-Analysis*, 11: 279–90.

1984b   'The autistic enclave'. *Bulletin of AGIP*. Private circulation.

1984c   'Autism – aetiology and therapy'. *Proceedings of the Paris Conference on Autism*.

1984d   'Significant understandings in attempts to ameliorate autistic states'. *Proceedings of the Monaco Conference on Autism*.

1984e   'The growth of understanding'. *Journal of Child Psychotherapy*, 10 (2): 137–49.

1985   'Autistic shapes and adult pathology'. *Topique*. France.

1985   'The threat of dissolution'. *Dedale*. France.

1987   'The rhythm of safety'. *Winnicott Studies*, 2.

1988   'The black hole – a significant element in autism'. *Free Associations*, 11.

1988   'Psychotherapy with children who cannot play'. *International Review of Psycho-Analysis*, 15.
1988   '"To be or not to be": a study of autism'. *Winnicott Studies*, 3.
1988   'What autism is and what autism is not'. In Rolene Szur and Sheila Miller (eds) *Extending Horizons*. London: Karnac.
1991   'Revised understandings of psychogenic autism'. *International Journal of Psycho-Analysis*, 72 (4): 585–92.
1993   'On psychogenic autism'. *Psychoanalytic Inquiry*, 13 (1): 34–41.
1994   'The perpetuation of an error'. *Journal of Child Psychotherapy*, 20 (1): 3–23.

BOOKS

1951   *A Group of Juniors: A Study of Latency Children's Play*. London: Heinemann Educational Books.
1972   *Autism and Childhood Psychosis*. London: Hogarth; New York: Jason Aronson (1973).
1981a *Autistic States in Children*. London and Boston: Routledge & Kegan Paul.
1986   *Autistic Barriers in Neurotic Patients*. London: Karnac; New Haven: Yale University Press.
1990   *The Protective Shell in Children and Adults*. London: Karnac.
1992   *Autistic States in Children*. London: Routledge. Revised edn.

VIDEOS

Five for Further Education Seminars (2 in London, 3 in Paris):

Dr Marion Solomon
1023 Westholme Avenue
Los Angeles
California 09924 USA

Two lectures for California Institute of the Arts:

Dr Jeannette Gadt
Dean of Division of Critical Studies
California Institute of the Arts
Bean Parkway
California 91355 USA

Hello Mrs Tustin. Interview for Hommage à Frances Tustin, Alès-en-Cevennes, France, 24–5 October 1992:

Dr Claude Alliona
L'Amounié
Pierregras 07460
St Andre du Cruzières
France

Bibliography

Alvarez, A. (1980) Two regenerative situations in autism: reclamation and becoming vertebrate. *Journal of Child Psychotherapy*, 6: 69–80.
—— (1992) *Live Company*. London and New York: Tavistock/Routledge.
Anthony, J. (1958) An experimental approach to the psychopathology of childhood autism. *British Journal of Medical Psychology*, 31(3, 4): 211–25.
—— (1973) Tustin in Kleinian land. Review of *Autism and Childhood Psychosis*. *Psychotherapy and Social Science Review*, 1(5): 14–22.
Arnold, M. (1852) Empedocles on Etna. In H. Newbolt (ed.) *Poems of Matthew Arnold*. London and Edinburgh: Nelson & Sons.
Balbirnie, R. (1985) Psychotherapy with a mentally handicapped boy. *Journal of Child Psychotherapy*, 11(2): 65–76.
Balint, M. (1968) *The Basic Fault: Therapeutic Aspects of Regression*. London: Tavistock.
Baron-Cohen, S. (1989) The autistic child's theory of mind: a case of specific developmental delay. *Journal of Child Psychology and Psychiatry*, 30(2): 285–97.
Baron-Cohen, S., Leslie, A. M. and Frith, U. (1985) Does the autistic child have a 'theory of mind'? *Cognition*, 21: 37–46.
Bazeley, E. T. (1928) *Homer Lane and the Little Commonwealth*. London: NEBC.
Bemperad, J. R. (1979) Adult recollections of a formerly autistic child. *Journal of Autism and Developmental Disorders*, 9 (2): 179–97.
Bender, L. (1969) Autism in children with mental deficiency. *American Journal of Mental Deficiency*, 64: 81–6.
Bennett, A. (1992) *The Madness of George III*. London and Boston: Faber & Faber.
Bettelheim, B. (1967) *The Empty Fortress: Infantile Autism and the Birth of the Self*. New York: Free Press.
Bibring, E. (1953) The mechanism of depression. In P. Greenacre (ed.) *Affective Disorders*. New York: International Universities Press.
Bick, E. (1964) Infant observation in psychoanalytic training. *International Journal of Psycho-Analysis*, 45: 558–66.
—— (1968) The experience of the skin in early object relations. *International Journal of Psycho-Analysis*, 49: 484–6.

Bion, W. R. (1957) Differentiation of the psychotic from the non-psychotic personalities. In *Second Thoughts: Selected Papers on Psychoanalysis*. New York: Jason Aronson.

—— (1962a) A theory of thinking. *International Journal of Psycho-Analysis*, 43. Also in W. R. Bion (1967) *Second Thoughts*. New York: Jason Aronson.

—— (1962b) *Learning from Experience*. London: Heinemann.

—— (1963) Elements of psychoanalysis. In *Seven Servants*. New York: Jason Aronson (1977).

—— (1965) *Transformations*. New York: Jason Aronson.

—— (1967) *Second Thoughts*. New York: Jason Aronson.

—— (1970) Attention and interpretation. In *Seven Servants*. New York: Jason Aronson (1977).

Bleuler, E. (1911) *Dementia Praecox or the Group of Schizophrenias*. (Trans.) J. Zinken (1950). New York: International Universities Press.

—— (1913) Autistic thinking. *American Journal of Insanity*, 69: 873–86.

Bollas, C. (1979) The transformational object. *International Journal of Psycho-Analysis*, 60: 97–108.

—— (1989) *Forces of Destiny*. London: Free Association Books.

Bower, T.G. (1971) The object in the world of the infant. *Scientific American*, 225: 30–38.

Bowlby, J. (1969) *Attachment and Loss*. Vol. 1: *Attachment*. New York: Basic Books.

—— (1973) *Attachment and Loss*. Vol. 2: *Separation, Anxiety and Anger*. London: Hogarth.

—— (1980) *Attachment and Loss*. Vol. 3: *Loss, Sadness and Depression*. London: Hogarth.

—— (1988) *A Secure Base: Clinical Applications of Attachment Theory*. London: Routledge.

Brouzet, E. (1674) 'Essai sur l'éducation médicinale des enfants et leurs remèdes.' Paris.

Cameron, J. L., Freseman, T. and McGhie, A. (1956) A clinical observation on chronic schizophrenia. *Psychiatry*, 19: 271–81.

Cameron, K. (1955) Psychosis in infancy and early childhood. *Medical Press*, 234: 28–83.

—— (1958) A group of twenty-five psychotic children. *Revue Psychiatrique Infantile*, 25: 117–22.

Carroll, L. (1865/1871) *Alice's Adventures in Wonderland; Alice Through the Looking Glass*. Combined vol. (1962). London: Puffin Books.

Clevinger, S. V. (1883) Insanity in children. *American Journal of Neurological Psychiatry*, 2: 585–601.

Cooray, S. (1993) Unpublished paper.

Creak, M. (1961) Schizophrenic syndrome in childhood: report of a working party. *British Journal of Medical Psychology*, 2: 869–90.

Creak, M. and Ini, S. (1960) Families of psychotic children. *Journal of Child Psychology and Psychiatry*, 1: 156–75.

De Meyer, M., Churchill, D., Pontius, W. and Gilkey, K. (1971) A comparison of five diagnostic systems for child schizophrenia and infantile autism. *Journal of Autism and Childhood Schizophrenia*, 1: 175–89.

De Sanctis, S. (1906) Sopra alcune varieta della demenza precoce. *Revista Sperimentale di Freniatria e di Medicina Legale*, 32: 141–65.

—— (1973) On some varieties of dementia praecox. In S. A. Szurek and I. N. Berlin (eds) *Clinical Studies in Childhood Psychosis*. New York: Brunner/ Mazel.

Diagnostic and Statistical Manual of Mental Disorders (1987) 3rd edn, rev. Washington, DC: American Psychiatric Association.

Eisenberg, L. (1956) The autistic child in adolescence. *American Journal of Psychiatry*, 112: 607–12.

—— (1966) Psychotic disorders in childhood. In R. E. Cook (ed.) *Biological Basis of Paediatric Practice*. New York: McGraw-Hill.

Eliot, T. S. (1909–62) Burnt Norton. In *Collected Poems*. London: Faber & Faber.

Escalona, S. K. (1953) Emotional development in the first year of life. In M. Senn (ed.) *Problems of Infancy and Childhood*. Packawack Lake, NJ: Foundation Press.

Esquirol, J. E. D. (1838) *Des maladies mentales*, vol. 1. Paris: Baillière.

Fonagy, P., Steele, H. and Steele, M. (1991a) Maternal representations of attachment during pregnancy predict the organisation of infant–mother attachment at one year of age. *Child Development*, 62: 891–905.

Fonagy, P., Steele, H., Steele, M., Moran, G. S. and Higgett, A. A. (1991b) The capacity for understanding mental states: the reflective self in parent and child and its significance for security of attachment. *Mental Health Journal*, 13(3): 200–17.

Fraiberg, S. (1980) *Clinical Studies in Infant Mental Health: The First Year of Life*. New York: Basic Books.

—— (1982) Pathological defenses in infancy. *Psychoanalytical Quarterly*, 51: 621–35.

—— (1987) *Selected Writings of Selma Fraiberg*. Columbus: Ohio State University Press.

Frazer, J. G. (1922) *The Golden Bough*. London: Macmillan.

Freud, S. (1900) *The Interpretation of Dreams*. SE, 4.

—— (1911) *Formulations on Two Principles of Mental Functioning*. SE, 12.

—— (1913) *Totem and Taboo*. SE, 8.

—— (1920) *Beyond the Pleasure Principle*. SE, 18.

—— (1923) *The Ego and the Id*. SE, 19: 19–27.

Frith, U. (1985) Recent experiments on autistic children's cognitive and social skills. *Early Child Development and Care*, 22: 237–57.

—— (1989) *Autism: Explaining the Enigma*. Oxford: Blackwell.

Gaddini, R. and Gaddini, E. (1959) Rumination in infancy. In L. Jessner and E. Pavenstedt (eds) *Dynamics of Psychopathology in Childhood*. New York: Grune & Stratton: 166–85.

Gage, J. (1987) *J. M. W. Turner: a Wonderful Range of Mind*. New Haven and London: Yale University Press.

Galloway, S. (1993) Unpublished paper.

Gillberg, C. (1985) Asperger's syndrome and recurrent psychosis – a neuro-psychiatric case study. *Journal of Autism and Developmental Disorders*, 15: 389–98.

—— (1988) The neurobiology of infantile autism. *Journal of Child Psychology and Psychiatry*, 29(3): 257–66.

—— (1990) Autism and pervasive developmental disorders. *Journal of Child Psychology and Psychiatry*, 31(1): 99–119.

Goldfarb, W. (1956) Receptor preferences in schizophrenic children. *American Medical Association: Archives of Neurological Psychiatry*, 76: 643–52.

Grandin, T. and Scariano, M. (1986) *Emergence Labelled Autistic*. Tunbridge Wells: Costello.

Grotstein, J. S. (1980) Primitive mental states. *Contemporary Psychoanalysis*, 16: 479–546.

—— (1981) *Splitting and Projective Identification*. New York: Jason Aronson.

—— (1985) The Schreber case revisited: schizophrenia as a disorder of self-regulation and of interactional regulation. *Yale Journal of Biology and Medicine*, 58(3): 299–314.

—— (1986) Schizophrenic personality disorder. In D. Feinsilver (ed.) *Towards a Comprehensive Model for Schizophrenic Disorders*. Hillsdale, NJ: Analytic Press.

—— (1987) Borderline as a disorder of self-regulation. In J. Grotstein, M. Solomon and J. Lang (eds) *The Borderline Patient: Emerging Concepts in Diagnosis, Psychodynamics and Treatment*. Hillsdale, NJ: Analytic Press.

—— (1989) The 'black hole' as the basic psychotic experience: some newer psychoanalytic and neuroscience perspectives on psychosis. *Journal of the American Academy of Psychoanalysis*, 6(3): 253–75.

Happe, F. and Frith, U. (1991) Is autism a pervasive developmental disorder? Debate and argument: How useful is the PDD label? *Journal of Child Psychology and Psychiatry*, 32(7): 1167–78.

Hawking, S. (1988) *A Brief History of Time*. London: Transworld Publishers.

Hedges, L. (1994) *The Organizing Experience*. New York: Jason Aronson (in press).

Hermelin, B. and O'Connor, N. (1970) *Psychological Experiments with Autistic Children*. Oxford: Pergamon Press.

Hobson, R. P. (1984) Early childhood autism and the question of egocentrism. *Journal of Autism and Developmental Disorders*, 14(1): 85–103.

—— (1985) Piaget: on ways of knowing in childhood. In M. Rutter and L. Hersov (eds) *Child and Adolescent Psychiatry: Modern Approaches*. Oxford: Blackwell.

—— (1986) The autistic child's appraisal of expressions of emotion. *Journal of Child Psychology and Psychiatry*, 27: 321–42.

—— (1989) Beyond cognition: a theory of autism. In G. Dawson (ed.) *Autism: Nature, Diagnosis and Treatment*. New York: Guilford.

Hoxter, S. (1972) A study of residual autistic conditions and its effects upon learning. *Journal of Child Psychotherapy*, 3(2).

International Classification of Diseases (1977) Geneva: WHO.

Joseph, B. (1975) The patient who is difficult to reach. In P. L. Giovanni (ed.) *Tactics and Technique in Psychoanalytic Therapy*, vol. 2. New York: Jason Aronson.

—— (1982) Addiction to near death. *International Journal of Psycho-Analysis*, 63: 449–56.

—— (1989) *Psychic Equilibrium and Psychic Change: Selected Papers of Betty Joseph*. (Ed.) M. P. Feldman and E. Spillius. London: Tavistock/Routledge.

Jung, C. G. (1919) *Psychology of the Unconscious*. London: Kegan Paul, Trench, Trubner & Co.

—— (1964) *Civilisation in Transition. Collected Works*, 10. (Trans.) R. F. C. Hull. London: Routledge & Kegan Paul.

Kanner, L. (1943) Autistic disturbances of affective contact. *Nervous Child*, 2: 217–50.

—— (1954) To what extent is early infantile autism determined by constitutional inadequacies? *Research Publications of the Association for Research in Nervous and Mental Disease*, 33: 378–85. Revised version in *Childhood Psychosis* (1973). Washington, DC: V. H. Winston & Sons.

—— (1959) The thirty-third Maudsley lecture: Trends in child psychiatry. *Journal of Mental Sciences*, 105: 581–93.

Kant, I. (1787) *The Critique of Pure Reason*. (Trans.) N. Kemp Smith (1929). London: Macmillan.

—— (1798) *The Classification of Mental Diseases*. (Trans. and ed.) T. Sullivan (1964). Doylestown, Pa.: Doylestown Foundation.

Kinston, W. and Cohen, J. (1986) Primal repression: clinical and theoretical aspects. *International Journal of Psycho-Analysis*, 67: 337–56.

Klein, M. (1930) The importance of symbol formation in the development of the ego. In *Love, Guilt and Reparation*. London: The Hogarth Press: 219–32.

—— (1946) Notes on some schizoid mechanisms. In *The Writings of Melanie Klein*, Vol. 3. London: The Hogarth Press.

Klein, S. (1980) Autistic phenomena in neurotic states. *International Journal of Psycho-Analysis*, 61: 395–402.

Kohut, H. (1977) *The Restoration of the Self*. New York: International Universities Press.

—— (1985) *The Analysis of the Self*. New York: International Universities Press.

Kohut, H. and Wolff, E. (1978) The disorders of the self and treatment: an outline. *International Journal of Psycho-Analysis*, 59: 413–24.

Kraepelin, E. (1896) *Dementia Praecox and Paraphrenia*. (Trans.) R. M. Barclay, (ed.) (1919) G. M. Robertson. Edinburgh: Livingstone.

Lacan, J. (1973) *The Four Fundamental Concepts of Psycho-Analysis*. (Trans.) A. Sheridan (1977). London: The Hogarth Press.

Laing, R. D. (1960) *The Divided Self*. London: Tavistock.

Leslie, A. M. (1987) Pretence and representation: the origins of 'theory of mind'. *Psychological Review*, 94: 412–26.

Leslie, A. M. and Frith, U. (1988) Autistic children's understanding of seeing, knowing and believing. *British Journal of Developmental Psychology*, 6: 315–24.

Mahler, M. (1949) Remarks on psychoanalysis with psychotic children. *Quarterly Journal of Child Behaviour*, 1: 18–21.

—— (1958) Autism and symbiosis, two extreme disturbances of identity. *International Journal of Psycho-Analysis*, 39: 77–83.

—— (1961) On sadness and grief in infancy and childhood: loss and restoration of the symbiotic love object. *Psychoanalytic Study of the Child*, 17: 332–51.

—— (1968) *On Human Symbiosis and the Vicissitudes of Individuation*. New York: International Universities Press.

—— (1985) in Proceedings of International Symposium on Separation-Individuation, Paris.

Mahler, M., Bergman, A. and Pine, F. (1975) *The Psychological Birth of the Human Infant*. New York: Basic Books.

Maudsley, H. (1879) *The Physiology and Pathology of Mind*. London: Macmillan. [Quotation from 1880 edn, where it was added in response to earlier criticisms.]

Meltzer, D. (1968) Terror, persecution, dread – a dissection of paranoid anxieties. *International Journal of Psycho-Analysis*, 49: 396–400.

Meltzer, D., Bremner, J., Hoxter, S., Weddell, H. and Wittenberg, I. (1975) *Explorations in Autism*. Strath Tay, Perthshire, Scotland: Clunie Press.

Meltzoff, A. N. (1981) Imitation, intermodal coordination and representation in early infancy. In G. Butterworth (ed.) *Infancy and Epistemology*. London: Harvester Press.

Meltzoff, A. and Barton, R. (1979) Intermodal matching in human neonates. *Nature*, 282: 403–4.

Meltzoff, A. and Moore, M. (1977) Imitations of facial and manual gestures by human neonates. *Science*, 198: 75–8.

Mental Health Act (1983) Chapter 20. London: HMSO.

Mercurialis, H. (1583) *De morbis puerorum*. Quoted in J. Ruhrah, *Paediatrics of the Past*. New York (1925).

Miller, J. (1978) *The Body in Question*. London: Jonathan Cape.

Miller, L., Rustin, M., Rustin, M. and Shuttleworth, J. (1989) *Closely Observed Infants*. London: Duckworth.

Mitrani, J. L. (1987) The role of unmentalised experience in the emotional etiology of psychosomatic asthma. Unpublished MS.

—— (1992) On the survival function of autistic manoeuvres in adult patients. *International Journal of Psycho-Analysis*, 73(2): 549–59.

Money-Kyrle, R. E. (1978) *Man's Picture of his World*. London: Duckworth. First published 1961.

Murray, L. (1992) The impact of maternal depression on infant development. *Journal of Child Psychology and Psychiatry*, 33(3): 543–61.

Murray, L. and Trevarthen, C. (1985) Emotional regulation of interactions between two month olds and their mothers. In T. M. Field and N. Fox (eds) *Social Perception in Infants*. New Jersey: Ablex.

Neill, A. S. (1968) *Summerhill*. Harmondsworth, Middlesex: Penguin Books.

Oesterreicher, S. (1540) *De infantium morborum diagnotione*. Basel.

Ogden, T. H. (1989) *The Primitive Edge of Experience*. Northvale, NJ: Jason Aronson.

O'Shaughnessey, E. (1992) Enclaves and excursions. *International Journal of Psycho-Analysis*, 73: 603–11.

Padel, J. (1978) Personal communication.

Penfield, W. and Rasmussen, T. (1950) *The Cerebral Cortex of Mind*. London: Macmillan.

Piaget, J. (1937a) *The Construction of Reality in the Child*. (Trans.) M. Cook (1952). New York: Basic Books.

—— (1937b) *The Origins of Intelligence in Children*. (Trans.) M. Cook (1952). New York: Basic Books.

Potter, H. W. (1933) Schizophrenia in children. *American Journal of Psychiatry*, 89: 1253–70.

Rank, B. (1949) Adaptation of psychoanalytic technique for treatment of young children with atypical development. *American Journal of Orthopsychiatry*, 19: 130–39.

Reid, S. (1990) The importance of beauty in the psycho-analytic experience. *Journal of Child Psychotherapy*, 16(1): 29–52.

Ricks, D. M. and Wing, L. (1975) Language, communication and the use of symbolism in normal and autistic children. *Journal of Autism and Childhood Schizophrenia*, 5: 191–221.

Riesenberg, Malcolm R. (1990) As-if: the phenomenon of not learning. *International Journal of Psycho-Analysis*, 71(3): 385–92.

Rose, S. A., Blank, M. S. and Bridger, W. H. (1972) Intermodal and intramodal retention of visual and tactual information in young children. *Developmental Psychology*, 6: 482–6.

Rosenfeld, H. A. (1950) Notes on the psychopathology of confusional states in chronic schizophrenia. *International Journal of Psycho-Analysis*, 31: 132–7.

—— (1971) A clinical approach to the psychoanalytic theory of the life and death instincts: an investigation into the aggressive aspects of narcissism. *International Journal of Psycho-Analysis*, 52: 169–78.

—— (1981) On the psychology and treatment of psychotic patients. In J. Grotstein (ed.) *Do I Dare Disturb the Universe?* Beverly Hills: Caesura Press.

—— (1987) *Impasse and Interpretation*. London: Tavistock.

Rutter, M. (1978) Diagnosis and definitions of childhood autism. *Journal of Autism and Developmental Disorders*, 8: 139–61.

—— (1979) Autism: psychopathological mechanisms and therapeutic approaches. In M. Borner (ed.) *Cognitive Growth and Development*. New York: Brunner/Mazel.

—— (1983) Cognitive deficits in the pathogenesis of autism. *Journal of Child Psychology and Psychiatry*, 24(4): 513–31.

—— (1985) The treatment of autistic children. *Journal of Child Psychology and Psychiatry*, 26: 193–214.

Rutter, M. and Schopler, E. (eds) (1978) *Autism: a Reappraisal of Concepts and Treatment*. New York and London: Plenum Press.

Sartre, J.-P. (1943) *Being and Nothingness*. (Trans.) H. E. Barnes (1957). London: Routledge & Kegan Paul.

Schultz, C. M. (1975) The meditations of Linus. *Peanuts Comic Strips*. London: Hodder & Stoughton.

Seguin, E. (1846) *Traitement moral des idiots*. Paris: Baillière.

Shapcote, E. (1927) Hymn 665. *The Church Hymnary*. Rev. edn. Oxford: OUP.

Sinason, V. (1986) Secondary mental handicap and its relationship to trauma. *Psychoanalytic Psychotherapy*, 2(2): 131–54.

——(1992) *Mental Handicap and the Human Condition*. London: Free Association Books.

Sohn, L. (1985a) Narcissistic organisation, projective identification and the formation of the identificate. *International Journal of Psycho-Analysis*, 66: 201–13.

—— (1985b) Anorexic and bulimic states of mind in the psycho-analytic treatment of anorexic/bulimic and psychotic patients. *Psychoanalytical Psychotherapy*, 1(2): 49–56.

Special Educational Need (1978). Report of the Committee of Enquiry into the Education of Handicapped Children and Young People. Chairman Mrs H. M. Warnock. London: HMSO.

Spensley, S. (1985a) Cognitive deficit, mindlessness and psychotic depression. *Journal of Child Psychotherapy*, 11(1): 35–50.

—— (1985b) Mentally ill or mentally handicapped? A longitudinal study of severe learning difficulty. *Psychoanalytical Psychotherapy*, 1(3): 55–70.

—— (1989) Psychodynamically oriented psychotherapy in autism. In C. Gillberg (ed.) *Diagnosis and Treatment of Autism*. New York and London: Plenum Press.

—— (1992) Seeing, believing, and concrete thinking: some commonalities in autism and obsessionality. Paper presented at Congrès Autisme Europe: The Hague.

Spillius, E. (1988) *Melanie Klein Today*, vol. 1, Introduction. London and New York: Routledge.

Spillius, E. and Feldman, M. (1989) *Psychic Equilibrium*. London and New York: Routledge.

Spitz, R. A. (1945) Hospitalism: an enquiry into the genesis of psychiatric conditions in early childhood. In O. Fenichel (ed.) *The Psychoanalytic Study of the Child*. Vol. 1: 53–74. New York: International Universities Press.

—— (1946) Anaclitic depression: an enquiry into the genesis of psychiatric conditions in early childhood. In O. Fenichel (ed.) *The Psychoanalytic Study of the Child*. Vol. 2: 313–42. New York: International Universities Press.

Steffenberg, S. and Gillberg, C. (1986) Autism and autistic-like conditions in Swedish rural and urban areas: a population study. *British Journal of Psychiatry*, 149: 81–7.

—— (1990) The etiology of autism. In C. Gillberg (ed.) *Autism, Diagnosis and Treatment*. New York: Plenum Press.

Steiner, J. (1987) The interplay between pathological organisations and the paranoid-schizoid position. *International Journal of Psycho-Analysis*, 68: 69–80.

—— (1991) A psychotic organisation of the personality. *International Journal of Psycho-Analysis*, 72(2): 201–7.

Stern, D. (1985) *The Interpersonal World of the Infant*. New York: Basic Books.

Symington, N. (1981) The psychotherapy of a subnormal patient. *British Journal of Medical Psychology*, 5(4): 187–99.

The Education Act (Handicapped Children) (1970). London: HMSO.

Warnock Report (1978) Report of the Committee of Enquiry into the Education of Handicapped Children and Young People. London: HMSO.

Williams, D. (1992) *Nobody Nowhere*. London: Doubleday.

Wing, L. (1981) Language, social and cognitive impairments in autism and severe mental retardation. *Journal of Autism and Developmental Disorders*, 11(1): 31–44.

—— (1988) The continuum of autistic characteristics. In E. Schopler and G. B. Mesibov (eds) *Diagnosis and Assessment of Autism*. New York: Plenum Press.

Wing, L. and Gould, J. (1979) Severe impairments of social interaction and associated abnormalities in children: epidemiology and classification. *Journal of Autism and Childhood Schizophrenia*, 9: 11–29.

Winnicott, D. W. (1956) Primary maternal preoccupation. In *Through Paediatrics to Psychoanalysis*. London: Hogarth Press (1975).
—— (1958) The capacity to be alone. In *The Maturational Processes and the Facilitating Environment*. London: Hogarth Press (1965).
—— (1960) Ego distortions in terms of true and false self. In *The Maturational Processes and the Facilitating Environment*. London: Hogarth Press (1965).
—— (1971) *Playing and Reality*. London: Tavistock.
Wolff, S. and Barlow, A. (1979) Schizoid personality in childhood: a comparative study of schizoid, autistic and normal children. *Journal of Child Psychology and Psychiatry*, 20: 29–46.

Index

Ackland, Sir R. 13
'adhesive identification' 4, 56, 69, 130
affect: significance of 20, 21
aloneness: autistic 22, 32
alpha function 54, 57, 69, 110, 130
Alvarez, A. 23, 51, 95, 125, 128
ambivalence 132
annihilation: fear of 24, 46, 60
Anthony, J. 23, 27
anxiety 56, 57–8, 69, 104, 125, 130; containment of 106, 127, 128; paranoid 62; primitive organismic 2, 94; and projection 124
Arnold, M. 123
attachment 16, 38, 48–9
autism: aetiology of 21, 27; and behaviourism and learning theory 18, 55, 105–7; and biology 2, 21; and bodily containment 4; and bodily separateness 24, 26, 53, 61, 78–81; characteristics of 18, 22, 76, 124–6; and child psychiatry 1; and childhood schizophrenia 31–2, 34, 37; and cognitive deficit 21, 27; as a defence 24, 27, 36; derivation of 1; discovery of 4, 17–18, 20–7, 90; Early Infantile 24, 32; and education 91–2; and hearing 3; and Kleinian child psychotherapy 17; and learning disability 95; and listening 125; and manual dexterity 64–6, 116; nature of 20–1; normal 24–7; and

organic cause of 34; and parental personalities 19; and pretend play 50; and psychoanalytic perspective 1, 55; and psychoanalytic treatment 1, 3, 95; and psychodynamic approach 21–2; psychogenic factors in 27, 34; and psychosis 1, 2, 22–3; as reaction to trauma 36, 53, 82; and schizophrenia 22; and sensory-dominated states 107, 111; and shape 26, 116; and Tustin's perspective on 1, 3, 4, 23–7, 34–6, 39, 50–4, 64–6, 70–2, 73–8, 111–12, 117, 127–8; and withdrawal 2, 18, 24, 27, 35, 36, 52
Autism and Childhood Psychosis (1972) 19, 22, 23–4
autistic aloneness 22, 32
autistic-contiguous position 56, 57, 58, 69
autistic disturbance: continuum of 22
'autistic features': and mental impairment 92
autistic objects 4, 64–5, 77–9, 130; concrete 65–6, 67
autistic rituals 48, 49
autistic sensation objects 27
autistic shapes 25, 70–2, 78, 131

baby observation 16
Balbirnie, R. 95
Balint, M. 47
Barlow, A. 22